Student Guide for
QuickBooks 2014

for

College Accounting

Fourteenth Edition

John Ellis Price
University of North Texas

M. David Haddock, Jr.
Chattanooga State Community College
Emeritus

Michael J. Farina
Cerritos College

Prepared by

Carol Yacht, M.A.
Software Consultant

Mc
Graw
Hill
Education

STUDENT GUIDE FOR QUICKBOOKS 2014
FOR COLLEGE ACCOUNTING, FOURTEENTH EDITION

Published by McGraw-Hill Education, 2 Penn Plaza, New York, NY 10121. Copyright © 2015 by McGraw-Hill Education. All rights reserved. Printed in the United States of America. Previous editions © 2012, 2009 and 2007. No part of this publication may be reproduced or distributed in any form or by any means, or stored in a database or retrieval system, without the prior written consent of McGraw-Hill Education, including, but not limited to, in any network or other electronic storage or transmission, or broadcast for distance learning.

Some ancillaries, including electronic and print components, may not be available to customers outside the United States.

This book is printed on acid-free paper.

2 3 4 5 6 7 8 9 0 ROV/ROV 1 0 9 8 7 6 5

ISBN: 978-0-07-763987-7
MHID: 0-07-763987-1

All credits appearing on page or at the end of the book are considered to be an extension of the copyright page.

The Internet addresses listed in the text were accurate at the time of publication. The inclusion of a website does not indicate an endorsement by the authors or McGraw-Hill Education, and McGraw-Hill Education does not guarantee the accuracy of the information presented at these sites.

www.mhhe.com

About the Author:

Carol Yacht is an accounting educator and textbook author. Carol is the author of McGraw-Hill's QuickBooks, Sage 50 (formerly Peachtree), and Microsoft Dynamics-GP textbooks. Carol also prepares the QuickBooks and Sage 50 Student Guides for use with McGraw-Hill's accounting textbooks (www.mhhe.com/yacht).

Carol taught on the faculties of California State University-Los Angeles, West Los Angeles College, Yavapai College, and Beverly Hills High School. To help students master accounting principles, procedures, and business processes, Carol includes accounting software in her classes.

An early user of accounting software, Carol Yacht started teaching computerized accounting in 1980. Yacht's teaching career includes first and second year accounting courses, accounting information systems, and computer accounting. Since 1989, Yacht's textbooks have been published by McGraw-Hill.

Carol contributes regularly to professional journals and is the Accounting Section Editor for *Business Education Forum*, a publication of the National Business Education Association. She is also the Editor of the American Accounting Association's Teaching, Learning, and Curriculum section's *The Accounting Educator*.

Carol Yacht was an officer of AAA's Two-Year College section and recipient of its Lifetime Achievement Award. She is an emeritus board member of the Microsoft Dynamics Academic Alliance, worked for IBM Corporation as an education instruction specialist, served on the AAA Commons Editorial Board, NBEA's Computer Education Task Force, and works for Intuit and Sage as an education consultant. She is a frequent speaker at state, regional, and national conventions.

Carol earned her MA degree from California State University-Los Angeles, BS degree from the University of New Mexico, and AS degree from Temple University.

Preface

The *Student Guide for QuickBooks 2014* shows you how to use QuickBooks 2014 software with selected end-of-chapter problems and mini practice sets from *College Accounting, 14e.* The transactions and instructions for each problem and mini-practice sets are included in the *Student Guide for QuickBooks 2014.* This includes QuickBooks screen illustrations, detailed steps for using the software, transactions for problem and mini-practice set completion, required steps for turning in reports, and the analysis component.

Refer to the QuickBooks 2014 Problem Correlation chart on pages xii-xiii to see which end-of-chapter problems work with QuickBooks 2014. In *College Accounting, 14e,* a **QB** icon is included to identify each end-of-chapter problem and mini practice set that have a QuickBooks company data file. In the *Student Guide,* company data files are called problem templates.

The software, QuickBooks 2014 Student Trial Edition Limited Use Only, is included with the *Student Guide for QuickBooks 2014.* The software has a time limit of 160 days and can be installed on an individual computer. A QuickBooks Templates CD is also included with the *Student Guide,* which includes problem template files with starting data.

SYSTEM REQUIREMENTS

The following systems requirements are online at http://accountants.intuit.com/accounting/quickbooks/accountant/. Select Tech Specs.

- Windows 8 (including 64-bit), 7 (including 64-bit), Vista (SP1 including 64-bit
- 2.0 GHz processor, 2.4 GHz recommended
- 1GB of RAM for a single user, 2 GB of RAM recommended for multiple users
- 2.5 GB available disk space (additional space required for data files)
- 60 MB disk space for Microsoft .NET 4.0 Runtime (provided on the QuickBooks CD)
- Minimum 1024x768 screen resolution. 16-bit or higher color
- 4x CD-ROM
- Product registration required, refer to pages vii-viii.
- 2GB or higher USB drive for backups

Integration with Other Software

- Microsoft Word and Excel integration requires 2003, 2007, or 2010 (including 64-bit).
- Synchronization with Outlook requires QuickBooks Contact Sync for Outlook 2003, 2007, and 2010 (including 64-bit; downloadable for free at: www.quickbooks.com/contact_sync)
- Email estimates, invoices and other forms with Gmail, Yahoo! Mail, windows Mail
- Compatible with QuickBooks Point of Sale version 10 and later

SOFTWARE INSTALLATION

The software included with the *Student Guide for QuickBooks 2014* is a 160-day single user copy of QuickBooks 2014 Student Trial Edition. The software can be installed on an individual computer, and must be registered within 30 days.

All the QuickBooks screen illustrations shown in the *Student Guide for QuickBooks 2014* were done with QuickBooks Accountant Edition 2014. To check the QuickBooks version, from the menu bar, select Help, About QuickBooks Accountant 2014.

To close, press <Esc> or click on the screen. You can also press the function key <F2> to see the version, release, and whether your software is registered. Your release number may differ.

If you have another version of QuickBooks installed on your computer, the author suggests deleting it. Refer to Appendix A, page 141, Uninstall QuickBooks.

Follow these steps to install the software on an individual computer.

1. Start your computer. Close all programs. If Microsoft Outlook or any Virus protection programs are open, close them, along with other programs that may be open. Disable antivirus program.
2. Insert The QuickBooks 2014 Student Trial Edition Limited Use Only CD into the CD drive.
3. If necessary, select Run setup.exe. (If Autorun is enabled, Setup will start automatically.) If a screen prompts to select <Yes> or <Continue>, do that. Be patient, it will take a few minutes for the installer to start.
4. The Welcome to QuickBooks! window appears. Click <Next>.

5. Accept the license agreement. Click <Next>.
6. Accept Express installation. Click <Next>.
7. Type the License and Product numbers shown on the CD envelope. Click <Next>.
8. The Ready to Install window appears. Review the information on this window. Click <Install>. If a While QuickBooks is installing, let's take care of your registration window appears, select <Skip this>. Steps for **Software Registration** are shown below.
9. When the Congratulations! window appears, select <Open QuickBooks>. Close the QuickBooks Setup window by clicking <X> on its title bar. Go to Chapter 4, page 1 or exit QuickBooks. To exit, select File, Exit.
10. Remove the CD.

Note to Instructors: For software installation in the school's computer lab or classroom, please refer to the Intuit Education Program at http://accountants.intuit.com/intuit-education-program. As of this writing, the cost for classroom site licenses is:

- 10 computers, $300*
- 25 computers, $460*
- 50 computers, $690*
  *(Pricing is subject to change)

These site licenses do not allow Multi-User Access. Multi-user mode means more than one person (up to five) work with a single company data file at the same time. Intuit Education Program site licenses for QuickBooks do not have this feature.

Classroom site licenses for QuickBooks 2014 are for one year. To order a classroom site license, call the Intuit Education Program, (866) 570-3843 (Monday through Friday, 6am to 2pm Pacific Time), or email education@intuit.com; http://accountants.intuit.com/intuit-education-program .

SOFTWARE REGISTRATION

Follow these steps to register QuickBooks 2014.

1. Start QuickBooks. If the QuickBooks Setup window appears, click on the <X> on its title bar to close it.
2. From the menu bar, select Help; Register QuickBooks. Select <Register>. If Register is not available on the Help menu, go to number 5 below.
3. The QuickBooks Registration - Create Login window appears. Follow the screen prompts to create an account and register.
4. When the QuickBooks Registration - Confirmation window appears, select <No Thanks, Start QuickBooks>. If necessary, close the Registration window.
5. To check your registration, press the function key <F2>. The Product Information window appears and displays REGISTERED. (*Hint:* OR, From the Icon bar, select 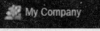. The Product Information window shows REGISTERED. If not,

register.) **Failure to complete registration within 30 days results in being locked out of the program.**

NO OPTICAL DRIVE (CD or DVD)

If your PC or laptop does <u>not</u> have a DVD or CD drive, go online to http://support.quickbooks.intuit.com/support/ProductUpdates.aspx to download QuickBooks Accountant 2014.

1. Link to <u>Visit the Install Center</u> to read installation steps.

2. If "Your product is **QuickBooks Accountant 2014**" is shown, select .

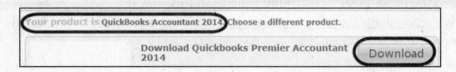

OR if QuickBooks Accountant 2014 is <u>not</u> shown, complete these steps:

   a. In the Select your product list, select QuickBooks Premier.
   b. In the Select your version list, select Accountant 2014.

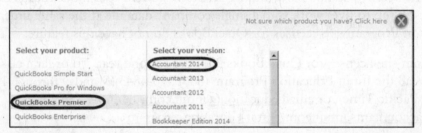

3. Click 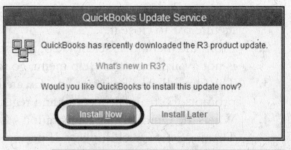. Use the License and Product Numbers included with the *Student Guide for QuickBooks 2014*. (Refer to the CD label on the inside front cover.) The License and Product numbers can be used one time.

NEW RELEASES OF QUICKBOOKS

When you start QuickBooks, a QuickBooks Update Service window may appear. The author suggests selecting . Because product updates fix QuickBooks issues, the author suggests installing the newer release. The QuickBooks Update Service window the release (R) number.

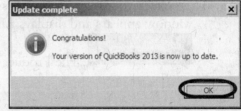

If a User Account Control window appears, click <Yes>. It will take a few minutes for the QuickBooks update. The Congratulations window appears. Click <OK>. An Updating window appears and QB opens. *If some of your screen images look different when compared to the illustrations in the Student Guide, you or the computer lab may not have updated QuickBooks.*

QUICKBOOKS TEMPLATES CD

The QuickBooks Templates CD includes the **problem templates** that are used to complete each problem shown in the *Student Guide for QuickBooks 2014*. The templates include starting data. The QuickBooks 2014 Problem Correlation chart on pages xii-xiii shows the file names. The detailed steps in the *Student Guide* show you how to restore each problem template file, complete the work with QuickBooks, and how to backup or save files.

IMPORTANT: Problem template files are upward but not downward compatible. This means that the problem template files can be used with QuickBooks 2014 and later versions, but not lower versions of QuickBooks (2013 and lower).

If your computer does not have a CD or DVD optical drive, the problem templates could be copied to a USB flash drive. To copy the problem templates from the QuickBooks Templates CD to a USB flash drive, use a computer in the classroom or another PC with an optical drive. To download QB 2014, refer to pages vii-viii, No Optical Drive (CD or DVD).

COPYING QUICKBOOKS PROBLEM TEMPLATES

Follow these steps to copy the QuickBooks problem templates from the CD included with the book.

1. Insert the QuickBooks Templates CD into your computer's CD drive. (The Templates CD is in an envelope on the back cover of the *Student Guide*.)
2. Drag the QuickBooks Problem Templates folder to your desktop; *or,* other location where you want the files to reside. The QuickBooks files that can be used with end-of-chapter problems are shown on pages xii-xiii.

CONVENTIONS USED

As you work through the problems in this book, you will be expected to read and follow the step-by-step instructions. Numerous screen illustrations guide your work.

The conventions used in this book are shown below.

1. Information that you type appears in boldface.

    Examples: Type **10/1/2016** in the Date field.
                Type **60000** in the Debit field.
2. Keys on the keyboard that should be pressed appear within greater and lesser signs.

    Examples: Press <Tab>
                Press <Enter>

---

3. Unnamed buttons and picture icons are shown as they appear.

Examples:

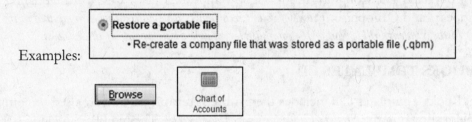

QUICKBOOKS FILE EXTENSIONS

QuickBooks includes file type choices for backing up. Backing up files is another name for saving. If needed, refer to Appendix A, How Do I Show File Extensions?, page 132.

Backup Files: QuickBooks Portable Company Files (.QBM)

In order to backup a file, the Create Copy feature is used. The backup files made in the *Student Guide* show how to use QuickBooks' portable company file feature. Portable files create a compact version of company data. The extension, .QBM, is automatically added to QuickBooks' portable company backup files. Detailed steps for backing up are on pages 12-13 (Create Copy or Backup), steps 1-6.

Restore Files: QuickBooks Working Files (.QBW)

In order to open a file, the Open or restore an existing company feature is used. When files are restored, QuickBooks creates a company file name with the extension .QBW (QuickBooks working file or company file). The default file name is the company name ending in the extension, .QBW. For example, the company file name for Problem 4-2A is Satillo Richey.QBW.

If the file was previously restored, the file name may include additional characters in addition to the company name. For example, let's say you are restoring the Problem 04.2A.Satillo Richey.QBM file. When you open the file, the company file name shows xxSatillo Richey.QBW (substitute the x's for other letters or numbers). The company file name is changed because Satillo Richey was previously restored. Detailed steps for starting QuickBooks and opening a company file are on pages 1-4 (Getting Started: Problem 4.2A), steps 1-8. Detailed steps for restoring files are on pages 13-14 (Open or Restore Company), steps 1-7.

QUICKBOOKS HOME PAGE

When you open a company in QuickBooks, the Home page appears. The QuickBooks Home page provides the big picture of how business tasks work together. Tasks are organized into groups—Vendors, Customers, Employees, Company, and Banking— with workflow arrows to help you learn how tasks relate to each other and to help you decide what to do next. The illustration on the next page shows QuickBooks' Home page.

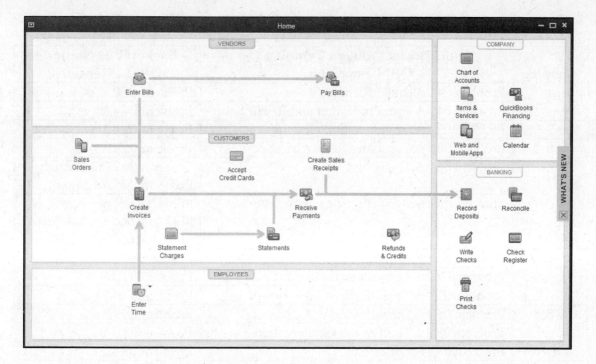

The workflow arrows indicate a progression of QB tasks. However, these arrows do not restrict you from doing tasks in a different order, or an order that works better for you.

When you use QuickBooks, return to the Home page by clicking **Home** on the Icon Bar. To start a task, simply click the icon for the task you want to do. For example, to see the company's chart of accounts, click Chart of Accounts.

Each icon includes a ToolTip so you can learn about the QuickBooks task associated with that icon. To open a ToolTip, place your mouse pointer over the icon. An explanation of the icon appears. The ToolTip for the chart of accounts icon is shown below.

> View and modify your QuickBooks accounts (bank, income, expense, etc.)

Clicking the icons on the Home page takes you to the window for that task. Some icons also include a drop-down arrow. In addition to the workflow diagram, the Home page provides company information and access to additional tasks on the right side pane.

QuickBooks 2014 Problem Correlation with *College Accounting, 14e*

Chapter	QuickBooks Problem Templates – QBM extensions	Backup File Names – QBM extensions
4	Problem 04.2A.Satillo Richey	Problem 04.2A
	Problem 04.4A.Farmers Market and Repair Shop	Problem 04.4A
5	Problem 05.4A.Judge Creative Designs	Problem 05.4A
6	Problem 06.1A.Consumer Research Associates	Problem 06.1A
	Problem 06.2A.The King Group	Problem 06.2A.Adjusted Problem 06.2A.Closed
	Mini Practice Set 1.Wells' Consulting Services	Mini Practice Set 1.January Mini Practice Set 1.Adjusted Mini Practice Set 1.Closed
7	Problem 07.1A.Best Appliances	Problem 07.1A
	Problem 07.2A.Towncenter Furniture	Problem 07.2A
	Problem 07.4A.Bella Floral Designs	Problem 07.4A
8	Problem 08.1A.Digital World	Problem 08.1A
	Problem 08.3A.The English Garden Shop	Problem 08.3A
	Problem 08.4A.Office Plus	Problem 08.4A
9	Problem 09.1A.Entertainment Inc	Problem 09.1A
	Problem 09.3A.Awesome Sounds	Problem 09.3A
	Problem 09.4A.Bike and Hike Outlet	Problem 09.4A
11	Problem 11.2A.Mark Consulting Company	Problem 11.2A
12	Problem 12.2A.Sean McConnell	Problem 12.2A
13	Problem 13.1A.Quality Hardwoods Company	Problem 13.1A
	Problem 13.5A.Victoria Company	Problem 13.5A.Adjusted Problem 13.5A.Reversed
	Mini Practice Set 2.The Fashion Rack	Mini Practice Set 2.October Mini Practice Set 2.Adjusted Mini Practice Set 2.Closed
15	Problem 15.1A.Montana Leather Products	Problem 15.1A.Adjusted Problem 15.1A
	Problem 15.2A.Lucero Company	Problem 15.2A.June 2017 Problem 15.2A.December 2016
	Problem 15.4A.Pullman Company	Problem 15.4A
16	Problem 16.2A.Dennis Company	Problem 16.2A
	Problem 16.5A.Reliable Company	Problem 16.5A
19	Problem 19.2A.Oatis and Thomas Angler's Outpost	Problem 19.2A
	Problem 19.4A.Larry's Antiques	Problem 19.4A
	Problem 19.5A.Adams Pharmacy	Problem 19.5A
20	Problem 20.4A.Denzel Corporation	Problem 20.4A
	Problem 20.5A.Jaguar Corporation	Problem 20.5A

Chapter	QuickBooks Problem Templates – QBM extensions	Backup File Names – QBM extensions
21	Problem 21.1A.Divad Corporation	Problem 21.1A
	Problem 21.3A.Solomon Corporation	Problem 21.3A
	Problem 21.4A.Willy Corporation	Problem 21.4A
22	Problem 22.1A.Carlie Services Inc	Problem 22.1A.2016 Problem 22.1A.2017
	Problem 22.4A.New Computer Technology, Inc	Problem 22.4A.Face Value Problem 22.4A.Bond Retirement
	Mini Practice Set 3.The Texas Company	Mini Practice Set 3.December Mini Practice Set 3.Adjusted Mini Practice Set 3.Closed
27	Problem 27.1A.SoCal Trailers Co	Problem 27.1A
TOTALS	**37 problem templates**	**49 backups**

All problem material is included in the *Student Guide to QuickBooks 2014*. This includes QuickBooks screen images, detailed steps for using the software, transactions for problem completion, required steps for turning in reports to your instructor, and the analysis component.

Table of Contents

<table>
<tr><td>**Chapter**
4</td><td># The General Journal and the General Ledger</td></tr>
</table>

In Chapter 4 of *College Accounting, 14e,* there are two QuickBooks 2014 problems.

➢ Problem 4.2A Satillo Richey: Journalizing and posting transactions.
➢ Problem 4.4A Farmers Market and Repair Shop: Journalizing and posting transactions.

The instructions that follow assume that QuickBooks 2014 is installed and that you are using the QuickBooks problem templates for the *first time.*

Chapter 4's QuickBooks activities demonstrate how to:

- Restore two QuickBooks problem templates.
- Enter transactions in the general journal; post to the general ledger.
- Print the journal and the general ledger.
- Complete Problem 4.2A and Problem 4.4A.

GETTING STARTED: PROBLEM 4.2A

Use the following instructions to start QuickBooks and restore the problem template. For purposes of this book, **problem templates** are defined as prestored data files that end in a .QBM extension. Files with .QBM extensions can be used with QuickBooks 2014 and higher versions.

The steps below assume you are starting QuickBooks and opening a company file for the first time. (*Hint:* The problem templates can be restored with QB 2014 and higher versions but <u>not</u> QB 2013 and lower versions.)

1. Double-click [icon]. If a screen prompts to register, refer to Software Registration, pages vii-viii. You can also open QuickBooks by selecting Start; All Programs, QuickBooks, QuickBooks Premier - Accountant Edition. If necessary, close the Let's get your business set up quickly! window. If a company opens, from the menu bar click File; Open or Restore Company, *or* File; Close Company. Go to step 3, page 2. Your steps may differ because a QuickBooks company had been opened previously.

    Troubleshooting: A No Company Open window appears. What should I do? Select Open or restore an existing company. Then, go to step 3, page 2.

2. From the No Company Open window, select Open or restore an existing company.

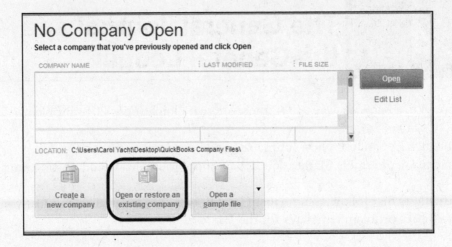

3. The Open or Restore Company window appears. Select Restore a portable file. If this is the first time you are using QB, a Warning screen appears that says "You have 160 days left to use your QuickBooks."

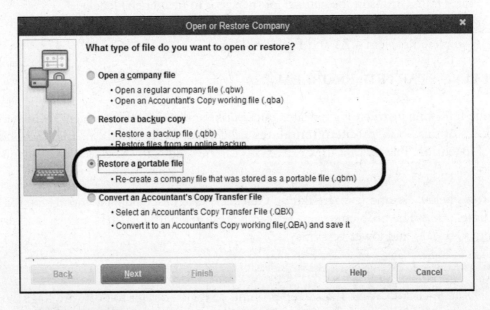

4. Click **Next**. The Open Portable Company File window appears. In the Look in field, go to the location of the QuickBooks Problem Templates folder. Select the the Problem 04.2A.Satillo Richey.QBM file. Observe that the File name field ends in the extension .QBM, and that the Files of type field shows QuickBooks Portable Company Files (*.QBM). Compare your Open Portable Company file window to the one shown on the next page.

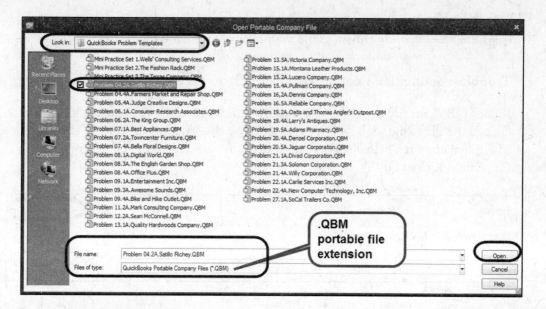

5. Click **Open**.

6. The Open or Restore a Company; Where do you want to restore the file? window appears.

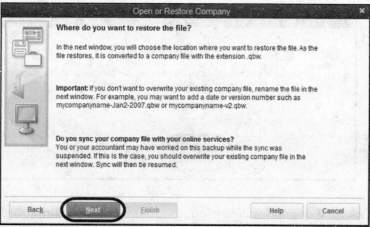

7. Click **Next**. The Save Company File as window appears. The Save in field shows the location where the company file is restored. If necessary, in the Save in field go to the appropriate location; *or,* accept the default location. **Note:** the File name ends in .QBW. QuickBooks company files end in a .QBW extension. QBW is an abbreviation for QuickBooks Working File.

---

8. Click . Be patient while the portable company file restores.

Troubleshooting: If a Confirm Save As window appears that says Satillo Richey.QBW already exits. Do you want to replace it? Click [No]. You could change the file name slightly. For example, type your intitials in front of the File name. The File name field below shows the author's initials before the company name - CY_Satillo Richey.QBW.

File name:	CY_Satillo Richey.QBW	▼	Save
Save as type:	QuickBooks Files (*.QBW)	▼	Cancel
			Help

Update Company

If QuickBooks was updated to a new release, an Update Company window may appear.

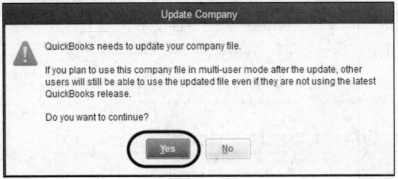

Click <Yes>. A Working window prompts Updating Data. Continue with step 9. If a Secuity Warning window appears, click <Yes>.

9. The screen prompts, The QuickBooks portable company file has been opened successfully; click [OK]. The title bar shows Satillo Richey – QuickBooks Accountant 2014. Your file is restored.

Troubleshooting:

a. If a Set Up an External Accountant User window appears, put a check mark in the box next to Don't show this again. Then, click <No>.

b. If the Accountant Center window appears, uncheck Show Accountant Center when opening a company file. Then click <X> on its title bar to close it. If necessary, from the Icon Bar, click 🏠 **Home** . The Home page appears.

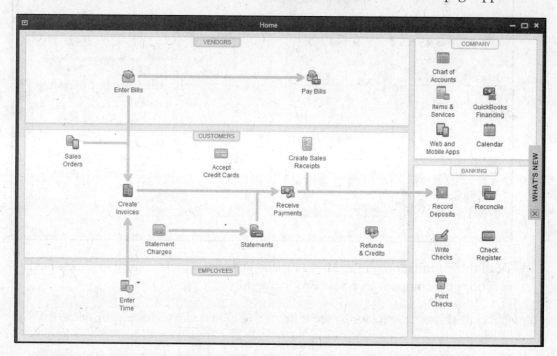

The QuickBooks Home page provides the big picture of how business tasks work together. Tasks are organized into groups—Vendors, Customers, Employees, Company, and Banking— with workflow arrows to help you learn how tasks relate to each other and to help you decide what to do next.

My Company

Before recording transactions for Satillo Richey, look at the My Company window included on the Problem 04.2A.Satillo Richey.QBM file. To look at My Company information, follow these steps.

1. The Satillo Richey Icon Bar should be displayed. From the Icon Bar, click **My Company** . The My Company window is shown on the next page. (*Hint:* You can also select My Company from the menu bar's Company selections.)

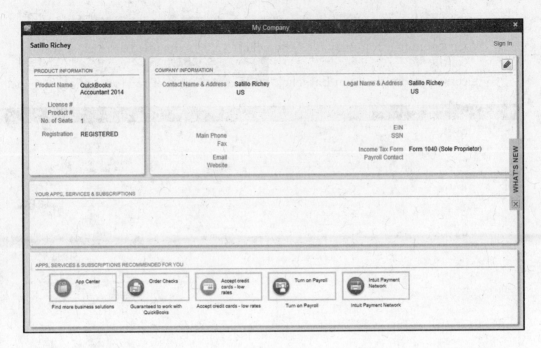

Read the information on the My Company window. The Income Tax Form field identifies the company as a Sole Proprietorship.

2. Check with your instructor to see if he or she would like to have your name on printouts. If this is the case, select the edit button, ✎. Then, add your first and last name to the Company Name field. Close the My Company window.

On October 1, 2016, Satillo Richey opened an advertising agency. He plans to use the chart of accounts shown below.

Satillo Richey Chart of Accounts

Problem 4.2A in *College Accounting, 14e*, includes general journal transactions for the month of October 2016. The data that you restored contains a chart of accounts for Problem 4.2A. Use these steps to display Satillo Richey's chart of accounts.

Instructions:

1. From the Home page, click ⌗ Chart of Accounts . (It is on the right side in the Company area.) *Or*, from the menu bar, click Lists; Chart of Accounts.
2. The Chart of Accounts window appears. You may need to enlarge the window to see the accounts. The chart of accounts shows account number and name, type, and balance total for each account that is used for journalizing and posting entries in the general journal.

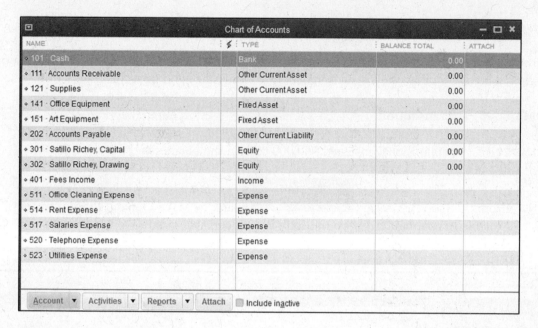

QuickBooks General Journal

QuickBooks provides three ways to journalize and post general journal entries. They are:

1. With the Chart of Accounts window open, click **Activities ▼** ; Make General Journal Entries.

   Or,

2. From the Icon Bar, select **👤 Accountant** . Within the Accountant Center, link to Make General Journal Entries. Read the Assigning Numbers to Journal Entries window. Then click on the box next to Do not display this message in the future. Click <OK> (*Hint:* If Accountant is not on the Icon Bar, from the menu bar, select Accountant, Accountant Center. Link to Make General Journal Entries.)

   Or,

3. From the menu bar, select Company; Make General Journal Entries. The instructions in this book demonstrate menu bar and Icon Bar selections.

The instructions that follow explain how to journalize and post the October 1 transaction in QuickBooks' general journal. For purposes of journalizing and posting journal entries, always use the dates shown. This ensures the proper order for posting entries to the general ledger.

After following the steps to journalize the October 1 transaction, journalize and post the October 2 through October 30, 2016 transactions. The October 2-30 transactions are shown on page 9-10.

Instructions:

On October 1, 2016, Satillo Richey opened an advertising agency. The October 1 transaction is shown below. Follow the instructions below to journalize and post this transaction.

Date   **Transaction**

10/1/2016   Satillo Richey invested $60,000 cash in the business.

1. From the Icon Bar, select 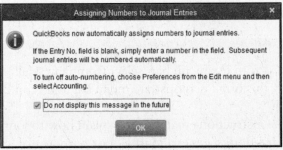 ; link to Make General Journal Entries. (*Hint:* If Accountant is not on the Icon Bar, select Accountant from the menu bar, then Accountant Center.)

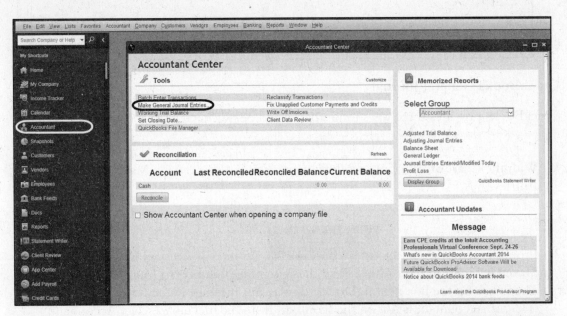

The Assigning Numbers to Journal Entries window may appear. Read the information. Click on the box next to Do not display this message in the future to place a checkmark in it. Click [OK] .

2. Type **10/1/2016** in the <u>D</u>ate field.
    (*Hint:* Typing **16** for the year is okay. You can also click on the calendar icon and select the date.) Press <Tab> two times. Uncheck Adjusting Entry – [ADJUSTING ENTRY] . Press <Tab>.

3. Your cursor is in the Account field. Type **101** and 101 Cash automatically appears in the Account column. Press <Tab>.
4. Type **60000** in the Debit column. Press <Tab> four times.
5. Your cursor is in the Account field. Observe that 60,000 is shown in the Credit column. Type **301** in the Account column. Press <Tab> three times to go to the Memo column.
6. Type **Beginning investment of owner** in the Memo field. (The author widened the Account column to show the full name of Account No. 301 Satillo Richey, Capital. To show this entry, click ⬤ Hide List .)

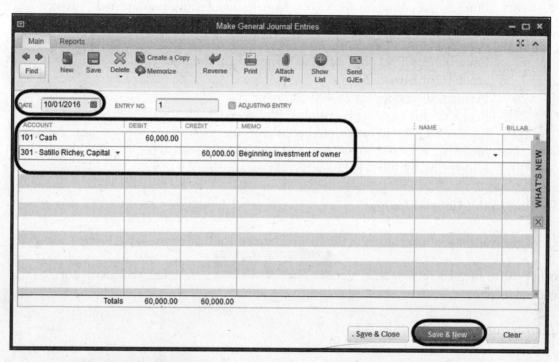

7. Click [Save & New].

8. The transactions for Problem 4.2A are shown below. Journalize and post the October 2-30 transactions. (*Hint:* You already entered the October 1 transaction, pages 8-9.)

Oct. 1 *Satillo Richey invested $60,000 cash in the business. (Hint: This transaction was journalized and posted on pages 8-9.)*
    2 Paid October office rent of $3,000; issued Check 1001.

Oct. 5 Purchased desks and other office furniture for $15,000 from Office Furniture Mart, Inc.; received Invoice 6704 payable in 60 days. (*Hint:* When the Tracking Fixed Assets on Journal Entries window appears, click on the box next to Do not display this message in the future to place a check mark in it. Click <OK> to close window.)

6 Issued Check 1002 for $3,200 to purchase art equipment.

7 Purchased supplies for $1,550; paid with Check 1003.

10 Issued Check 1004 for $600 for office cleaning service.

12 Performed services for $4,100 in cash and $1,900 on credit. (Use a compound entry.)

15 Returned damaged supplies for a cash refund of $400.

18 Purchased a computer for $3,000 from Office Furniture Mart, Inc., Invoice 7108; issued Check 1005 for a $1,750 down payment, with the balance payable in 30 days. (Use one compound entry.)

20 Issued Check 1006 for $7,500 to Office Furniture Mart, Inc., as payment on account for Invoice 6704.

26 Performed services for $4,400 on credit.

27 Paid $325 for monthly telephone bill; issued Check 1007.

30 Received $3,700 in cash from credit customers.

30 Mailed Check 1008 to pay the monthly utility bill of $400.

30 Issued Checks 1009–1011 for $8,000 for salaries.

Posting to the General Ledger

Once the transaction is recorded in the Make General Journal Entries window, the next step is to post to the general ledger. When [Save & New] is selected, you are posting to the general ledger.

Instructions:

1. The Make General Journal Entries window is ready for the October 2, 2016 transaction. Observe that the Entry No. field shows 2. Journalize and post the October 2, 2016 through October 30, 2016 transactions shown above. To change the Date field, type the appropriate date; *or* click the calendar icon [icon], then select the appropriate day of the month. *Remember to click* [Save & New] *after each transaction to post to the general ledger.*

2. When you record the last transaction, click [Save & Close] to post to the general ledger.

3. Click [x] on the Make General Journal Entries title bar to close the Make General Journal Entries window.

Printing the Journal

1. From the menu bar, select Reports, Accountant & Taxes, and Journal. Press <Tab> to go to the From field. Type **10/1/2016** in the From field. Press <Tab>.

2. Type **10/31/2016** in the To field. Click [Refresh]. Each journal entry recorded and posted from October 1 through 31, 2016 is shown. Observe which accounts are debited and credited. If you need to make a correction you can zoom (drill down) to the original entry by clicking on that line. For instance, move your cursor over 60,000.

Debit	◇
60,000.🔍	

   The cursor changes to a magnifying glass icon with a Z in it ( ). Double-click 60,000 and the 101 – Cash window appears. If you need to change the entry, type the correct amount and, if necessary, select the correct account. Click [Record] to make the change. Close the 101 – Cash window when you are through.

3. To print the Journal, click [Print]; then Report or Save as PDF. (*Hint:* If you select Save as PDF, type a file name; for example, Problem 4.2A.Journal. Then, go to the location to save your PDF file.)

4. If you select Report, the Print Reports window appears. Click [Print]. *Or,* click [Preview] to view the report on your monitor.

5. Close the Journal window by clicking [×] on its title bar. If a Memorize Report window appears, click on the box next to Do not show this message again; click [No].

Printing the General Ledger

1. From the Accountant Center, select General Ledger.
2. Press <Tab> to go to the From field. Type From field. Type **10/1/2016** in the From field. Press <Tab>.
3. Type **10/31/2016** in the To field. Click [Refresh]. The General Ledger report displays.
4. To print the General Ledger, click [Print]; Report. (Or you can save as a PDF file.)
5. The Print Reports window appears. Click [Print] or [Preview].
6. Close the General Ledger window by clicking <X> on the its title bar.

Analyze: What is the balance of account 202 in the general ledger? Use a blank piece of paper or the *Working Papers* to answer the analysis question.

QuickBooks Reports as Excel or PDF Files

Your instructor may want you to attach QuickBooks assignments to an email. Refer to page 138, Appendix A, Troubleshooting and QuickBooks Tips, Use Excel with QuickBooks, or E-mail Report as a PDF File.

Create Copy or Backup

Before you end work *or leave the computer lab*, remember to back up. When you back up data in QuickBooks, you are saving to that point. QuickBooks backup files are identified with the extension .QBM. This is the *same* extension as the QuickBooks problem templates. The following instructions show how to back up data. You may back up to the hard drive, network location, or external media. If necessary, substitute the appropriate drive letter for the location of your back up. Refer to the chart on pages xii and xiii for backup file names.

Instructions:

1. From the menu bar, click File, Create Copy. Select Portable company file. Compare your Save Copy or Backup window to the one shown below.

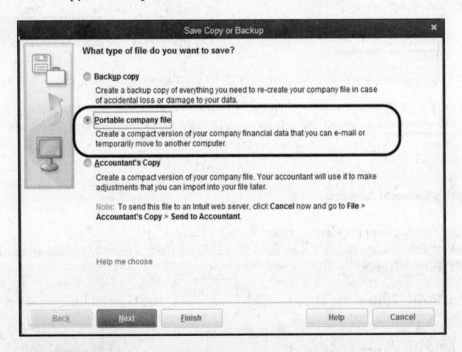

2. Click ![Next]. If necessary, go to the location where you want to save the file. (*Hint:* Insert a USB drive and save to external media. In the Save in field, select the location of your USB drive.)
3. In the File name field, type **Problem 04.2A**.

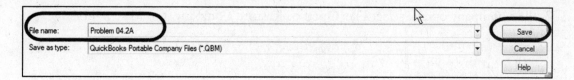

Observe that the Save as type field shows QuickBooks Portable Company Files(*.QBM). The extension, .QBM, is automatically added to portable files.

4. Click 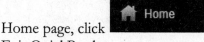.

5. When the Close and reopen window appears, read the information. Then click **OK**. A window prompts Creating Portable Company File. Please wait. When the QuickBooks information window appears, read it. The QuickBooks Information window tells you the location where you backed up (saved) the file. Click **OK**.

6. You are returned to the Satillo Richey – QuickBooks Accountant 2014. To see the Home page, click **Home**.

7. Exit QuickBooks.

Open or Restore an Existing Company

Once you back up, you can use QuickBooks Open or restore an existing company selection to start where you left off the last time you used QuickBooks. QuickBooks restore allows you to retrieve information that was previously saved or backed up. Restore is also used to open the QuickBooks problem templates.

If you are continuing work on your own PC or laptop, you do not need to restore. When a company opens, select File; Close Company. The No Company Open window shows Satillo Richey.QBW. Continue work by selecting .

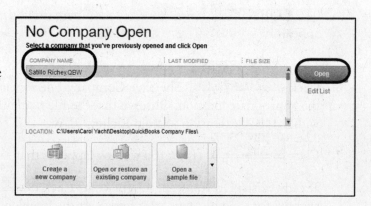

The steps below show how to restore the Problem 04.2A.QBM file. This is the file that you saved when you completed Problem 4.2A. The chart on pages xii and xiii shows the backup file names.

1. Start QuickBooks. If a QuickBooks Update Service window appears, the author suggests selecting **Install Now**.

2. If a company opens, select File; Open or Restore Company. Go to step 4 below.

3. Select 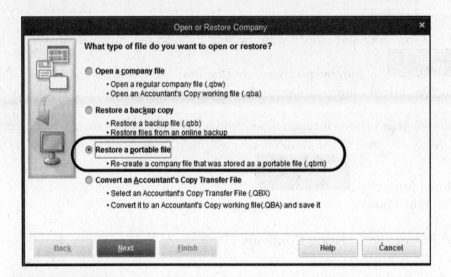.

4. The Open or Restore Company; What type of file do you want to open or restore? window appears. Select Restore a portable file.

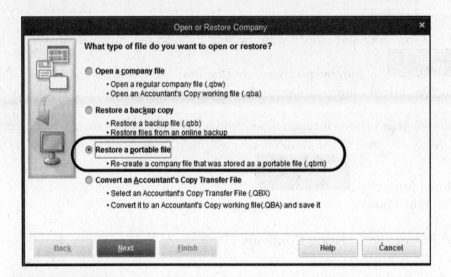

5. Click **Next**. The Open Portable Company File window appears. If necessary, go to the location of your backup file. Select the file; for example Problem 04.2A.QBM. Click **Open**. The Where do you want to restore the file? window appears.

6. Click **Next**. The Save Company File as window appears. If necessary, go to the appropriate location. Observe that the file name field shows the company name with a .QBW extension –Satillo Richey.QBW.

7. Click **Save**. (*Hint:* If a window appears that says Satillo Richey.QBW file already exists. Do you want to replace it? Click **No**. Change the file name slightly; for example, type your initials or the problem number in front of the file name.) Be patient while the portable file is being restored. It may take several minutes.

GETTING STARTED: PROBLEM 4.4A

Use the following instructions to start QuickBooks and restore the Problem 04.4A.Farmers Market and Repair Shop.QBM file.

Instructions:

1. Start QuickBooks.
2. If the menu bar shows a company name, click File; Open or Restore Company.
3. The Open or Restore Company window appears. Select Restore a portable file.

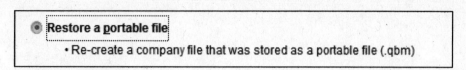

4. Click [Next]. The Open Portable Company File window appears. In the Look in field, go to the appropriate location for the Problem 04.4A.Farmers Market and Repair Shop.QBM file. Click on the file to highlight it. Click [Open]. (*Hint:* You can also double-click on the file name.)
5. The Open or Restore Company window appears. Click [Next].
6. The Save Company File as window appears. Accept the default file name or change it slightly. Click [Save]. (*Hint:* If a window appears saying the Farmers Market and Repair Shop.QBW file already exists, click No. Change the file name slightly. Then click Save.) If an Update Company window appears, click [Yes]. When the window prompts that the file has been opened successfully, click [OK]. When the Farmers Market and Repair Shop – QuickBooks Accountant 2014 appears, the file is restored.

My Company

Before recording transactions for Farmers Market and Repair Shop, look at the My Company information included on the Problem 04.4A.Farmers Market and Repair Shop.QBM file.

1. From the Icon Bar, select [My Company]. (*Or,* from the menu bar, select Company; My Company.) Read the information on the My Company window. Observe that the Income Tax Form field identifies the company as a Sole Proprietor.

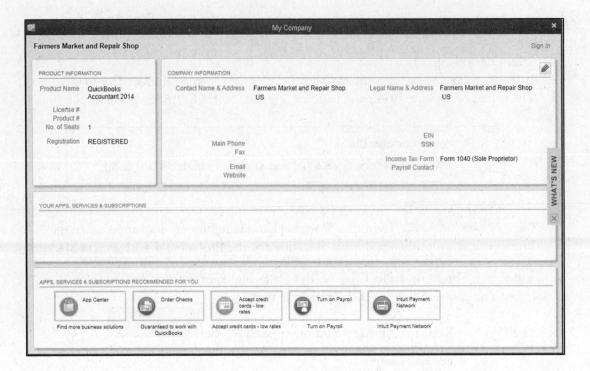

2. Check with your instructor to see if he or she would like to have your name on printouts. If so, click 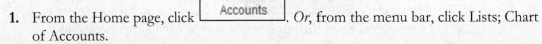 to add your first and last name to the Company Name field. Then, close the My Company window.

Farmers Market and Repair Shop's Chart of Accounts

Problem 4.4A in *College Accounting, 14e*, includes general journal transactions for the month of November 2016. The data that you restored contains a chart of accounts for Problem 4.4A. Use these steps to display Farmers Market and Repair Shop's chart of accounts.

Instructions:

1. From the Home page, click [Chart of Accounts]. *Or,* from the menu bar, click Lists; Chart of Accounts.
2. The Chart of Accounts window appears. Compare the chart of accounts to the one shown on the next page.

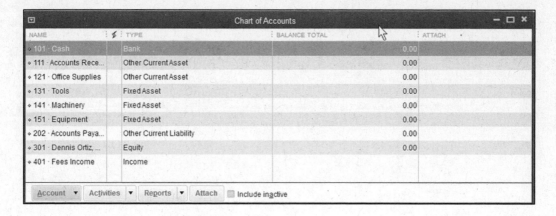

Journalizing and Posting Transactions

Four transactions for Farmers Market and Repair Shop that took place in November 2016 appear below. The general ledger accounts are shown on Farmers Market and Repair Shop's chart of accounts. Record the following November 1-20, 2016 transactions in the general journal

Nov. 1 Dennis Ortiz invested $55,000 in cash plus tools with a fair market value of $2,000 to start the business.

2 Purchased equipment for $2,050 and supplies for $550 from Office Depot, Invoice 501; issued Check 100 for $700 as a down payment with the balance due in 30 days.

10 Performed services for Hazel Sneed for $2,900, who paid $1,000 in cash with the balance due in 30 days.

20 Purchased machinery for $4,000 from Craft Machinery, Inc., Invoice 709; issued Check 101 for $1,500 in cash as a down payment with the balance due in 30 days.

Required:

1. Journalize and post each transaction in the general journal. Refer to the November 1-20 transactions.
2. Print the journal from November 1 through November 20, 2016. (Accountant Center; Journal Entries Entered/Modified Today. From 11/1/2016 to 11/30/2016.)
3. Print the general ledger. (*Hint:* In QuickBooks, credit balances have a minus sign in front of them.)
4. Back up. The suggested file name is **Problem 04.4A.QBM**.
5. **Analyze:** What liabilities does the business owe as of November 30? Use a blank piece of paper or the *Working Paper*s to answer the analysis question.

Chapter 5

Adjustments and the Worksheet

In Chapter 5 of *College Accounting, 14e*, there is one QuickBooks problem.

➤ Problem 5.4A Judge Creative Designs: Preparing a worksheet and financial statements, journalizing adjusting entries, and posting to ledger accounts.

The instructions assume that you are using the QuickBooks problem template for the *first time*.

Chapter 5's QuickBooks activities demonstrate how to:

- Restore one QuickBooks problem template.
- Print the January 31, 2016 trial balance.
- Journalize and post adjusting entries.
- Print the journal and the general ledger.
- Print the income statement and balance sheet.
- Complete Problem 5.4A.

GETTING STARTED: Problem 5.4A

Use the following instructions to start QuickBooks and restore the Problem 05.4A.Judge Creative Designs.QBM file.

Instructions:

1. Start QuickBooks.
2. If the menu bar shows a company name, click File; Open or Restore Company.
3. The Open or Restore Company window appears. Select Restore a portable file.
4. Click  . The Open Portable Company File window appears. In the Look in field, go to the appropriate location for the Problem 05.4A.Judge Creative

   Designs.QBM file. Click on the file to highlight it. Click **Open** . (*Hint:* You can also double-click on the file name.)

5. The Open or Restore Company window appears. Click **Next** .
6. The Save Company File as window appears. Accept the default file name or change it

   slightly. Click **Save** . (*Hint:* If a window appears saying the Judge Creative Designs.QBW file already exists, click <No>. Change the file name slightly. Then click <Save>.) When Judge Creative Designs – QuickBooks Accountant 2014 appears, the file is restored.

My Company

Before recording transactions for Judge Creative Designs, look at the My Company information included on the Problem 05.4A.Judge Creative Designs.QBM file.

1. From the Icon Bar, select ![My Company]. (*Or,* from the menu bar, select Company; My Company.) The My Company window appears.

2. Check with your instructor to see if he or she would like to have your name on printouts. Click ![pencil icon]. Add your first and last name to the Company Name field. Close the My Company window.

Displaying Judge Creative Designs Trial Balance

Follow these steps to see QuickBooks' trial balance. Use the information on QB trial balance to complete work.

Paula Judge owns Judge Creative Designs. The trial balance of the firm for January 31, 2016, the first month of operations, is shown below.

1. From the Icon Bar, select ![Reports]. In the list, select Accountant & Taxes. In the Account Activity area, select Trial Balance. Select or type **1/1/2016** to **1/31/2016** in the Dates field. (*Hint:* Click on the displayed date to highlight it, then type or select the appropriate date.)

2. Click ![Run].

3. The January 31, 2016 Trial Balance appears.

4. To print the Trial Balance, click ![Print]; Report.

5. The Print Reports window appears. Click 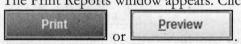 or . Compare your trial balance with the one shown on the next page.

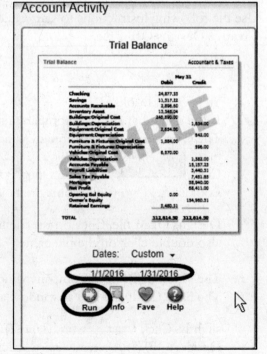

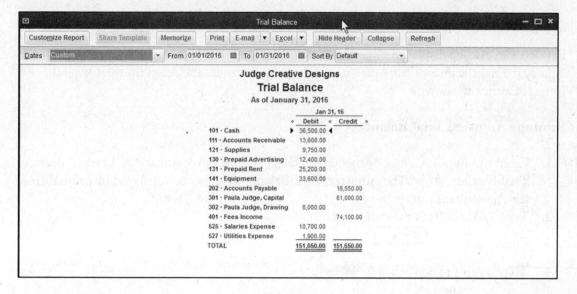

6. Click [×] to close the Trial Balance and return to the Home page.

Instructions

Paula Judge owns Judge Creative Designs. The trial balance of the firm for January 13, 2016, the first month of operations, is shown above.

1. Journalize and post the adjusting entries. (*Hint:* Date the adjusting entries January 31, 2016. Click on the box next to Adjusting Entry on the Make General Journal Entries window - [✓ ADJUSTING ENTRY]. Type **Adjustment a., b., c., d.** in the Memo field.)

   a. Supplies were purchased on January 1, 2016; inventory of supplies on January 31, 2016, is $1,600.
   b. The prepaid advertising contract was signed on January 1, 2016, and covers a four-month period.
   c. Rent of $2,100 expired during the month.
   d. Depreciation is computed using the straight-line method. The equipment has an estimated useful life of 10 years with no salvage value.

2. Print the January 31, 2016 journal.
3. Print the 1/1/2016 to 1/31/2016 Adjusted Trial Balance. (*Hint:* From the menu bar, select Reports; Accountant & Taxes, Adjusted Trial Balance. In order for an Adjusted Trial Balance to print, you need to check the Adjusting Entry field on the Make General Journal Entries window.)

Required

Reports can also be displayed or printed from the menu bar. Follow these steps to print the Adjusted Trial Balance. (*Hint:* Make sure Adjusting Entry was selected on the General Journal Entries window.)

Print the Adjusted Trial Balance

1. From the Report Center or menu bar, select Reports; Accountant & Taxes, Adjusted Trial Balance. (*Hint:* The Adjusted Trial Balance can also be displayed or printed from the Accountant Center.)
2. Type **1/31/2016** as the date.
3. Click <Run> or Refresh . The Adjusted Trial Balance displays.
4. To print of preview, click Print... .

Printing the Profit & Loss Statement and Balance Sheet

When using QuickBooks, the adjusting entries are journalized and posted *before* printing the profit & loss statement and balance sheet. (*Hint:* In QuickBooks, an income statement is called profit & loss.)

Substitute QuickBooks' balance sheet capital section for the statement of owner's equity. This is explained in step 2 below.

1. Follow these steps to print the profit & loss statement.

    a. From the Repot Center or menu bar, click Reports; Company & Financial, Profit & Loss Standard.
    b. Type **1/1/2016** to **1/31/2016** as the date.
    c. Click <Run> or Refresh .
    d. Click Print... to print or display the profit & loss report.
    e. Click ✕ to close the Profit & Loss window.

2. Follow these steps to print the balance sheet.

    a. From the Report Center or menu bar, click Reports; Company & Financial, Balance Sheet Standard.
    b. Type **1/31/2016** as the date.
    c. Click <Run> or Refresh .
    d. Click Print... to print or display the balance sheet.

e. Click ☒ to close the Balance Sheet window. (*Or*, if you did not close the Profit & Loss window, from the menu bar click Window, Close All. This also closes the Home page.)

QuickBooks' balance sheet reports separate balances for Capital, Drawing, and Net Income. In QuickBooks, Total Equity is computed as follows: Paula Judge, Capital minus Drawing, plus Net Income—60,000-8,000+47,870=100,870. (QuickBooks' balance sheet Equity section can be substituted for the textbook's statement of owner's equity.) In the textbook balance sheet, Paula Judge, Capital is reported as the result of three accounts (Paula Judge, Capital, minus Paula Judge, Drawing; plus Net Income).

3. Print the January 31, 2016 journal.
4. Print the January 1 to January 31, 2016 general ledger.
5. Back up. The suggested file name is **Problem 05.4A.QBM.**
6. **Analyze:** If the adjusting entries had not been made for the month, would net income be overstated or understated? Use a blank piece of paper or the *Working Paper*s to answer the analysis question.

Chapter 6

Closing Entries and the Postclosing Trial Balance

In Chapter 6 of *College Accounting, 14e*, there are three QuickBooks problems.

➤ Problem 6.1A Consumer Research Associates: Adjusting and closing entries.
➤ Problem 6.2A The King Group: Journalizing and posting adjusting and closing entries and preparing a postclosing trial balance.
➤ Mini Practice Set 1 Wells' Consulting Services: Service business accounting cycle.

The instructions that follow assume that QuickBooks 2014 is installed and that you are using the QuickBooks problem templates for the *first time*.

Chapter 6's QuickBooks activities demonstrate how to:

• Restore three QuickBooks problem templates.
• Journalize and post adjusting and closing entries.
• Print the journal and general ledger.
• Print the postclosing trial balance.
• Print financial statements.
• Complete Problem 6.1A, Problem 6.2A, and Mini-Practice Set 1.

GETTING STARTED: Problem 6.1A

Use the following steps to start QuickBooks and restore the Problem 06.1A.Consumer Research Associates.QBM file.

Instructions:

1. Start QuickBooks.
2. If the menu bar shows a company name, click File; Open or Restore Company.
3. The Open or Restore Company window appears. Select Restore a portable file.
4. Click [Next]. The Open Portable Company File window appears. In the Look in field, go to the appropriate location for the Problem 06.1A.Consumer Research Associates.QBM file. Click on the file to highlight it. Click [Open]. (*Hint:* You can also double-click on the file name.)
5. The Open or Restore Company window appears. Click .

6. The Save Company File as window appears. Accept the default file name or change it slightly. Click [Save]. When Consumer Research Associates - QuickBooks Accountant 2014 appears, the file is restored.

7. Continue with the next section "My Company."

My Company

Before recording transactions for Consumer Research Associates, look at the My Company information included on the Problem 06.1A.Consumer Research Associates.QBM file.

1. From the Icon Bar, select [My Company]. (*Or,* from the menu bar, select Company; My Company.) The My Company window appears.

2. To add your name to the Company Name field, click [✐]. Close the My Company window.

Consumer Research Associates Trial Balance (Adjusted)

Before journalizing and posting closing entries, display or print the trial balance. The revenue and expense account balances are *after* adjustments. For QuickBooks, this means that you will use this information to complete closing entries.

Consumer Research Associates, owned by Sam Hill, is retained by large companies to test consumer reaction to new products. On January 31, 2016, the firm's worksheet showed the following adjustments data: (a) supplies used, $2,340; (b) expired rent, $13,000; and (c) depreciation on office equipment $4,580. The balances of the revenue and expense accounts listed in the Income Statement section of the worksheet and the drawing account listed in the Balance Sheet section of the worksheet are shown on page 27.

Follow these steps to display or print the trial balance.

1. From the menu bar, select Reports; Accountant & Taxes, Trial Balance. (*Hint:* Trial balance can also be printed from the Report Center.)
2. Type **1/31/2016** in the From and To fields.
3. Click [Refresh]. Compare your trial balance to the one shown on the next page. The trial balance shown on page 27 is the adjusted trial balance. The Problem 06.1A.Consumer Research Associates.QBM file includes the account balances shown on the adjusted trial balance.

Consumer Research Associates
Trial Balance
As of January 31, 2016

	Jan 31, 16	
	Debit	Credit
101 · Cash	15,000.00	
121 · Supplies	4,680.00	
131 · Prepaid Rent	26,000.00	
141 · Office Equipment	25,000.00	
142 · Accum. Deprec.-Office Equipment		4,580.00
301 · Sam Hill, Capital		59,510.00
302 · Sam Hill, Drawing	11,000.00	
401 · Fees Income		100,000.00
511 · Deprec. Expense-Office Equip	4,580.00	
514 · Rent Expense	13,000.00	
517 · Salaries Expense	49,500.00	
520 · Supplies Expense	2,340.00	
523 · Telephone Expense	1,350.00	
526 · Travel Expense	10,390.00	
529 · Utilities Expense	1,250.00	
TOTAL	164,090.00	164,090.00

4. Compare this information to the revenue and expense account balances shown below.

REVENUE AND EXPENSE ACCOUNTS

401 Fees Income	$100,000 Cr.
511 Depr. Expense—Office Equipment	4,580 Dr.
514 Rent Expense	13,000 Dr.
517 Salaries Expense	49,500 Dr.
520 Supplies Expense	2,340 Dr.
523 Telephone Expense	1,350 Dr.
526 Travel Expense	10,390 Dr.
529 Utilities Expense	1,250 Dr.

DRAWING ACCOUNT

302 Sam Hill, Drawing	11,000 Dr.

Required:

1. Journalize and post the closing entries. (Use the revenue and expense account balances to complete the closing entries.)
2. Print the January 31, 2016 journal.
3. Back up. The suggested file name is **Problem 06.1A.QBM**.
4. **Analyze:** What closing entry is required to close a drawing account? Use a blank piece of paper or the *Working Paper*s to answer the analysis question.

GETTING STARTED: Problem 6.2A

Follow the steps below to restore the Problem 06.2A.The King Group.QBM file.

Instructions:

1. Start QuickBooks.
2. If the menu bar shows a company name, click File; Open or Restore Company.
3. The Open or Restore Company window appears. Select Restore a portable file.
4. Click [Next]. The Open Portable Company File window appears. In the Look in field, go to the appropriate location for the Problem 06.2A.The King Group.QBM file. Click on the file to highlight it. Click [Open]. (*Hint:* You can also double-click on the file name.)
5. The Open or Restore Company window appears. Click [Next].
6. The Save Company File as window appears. Accept the default file name or change it slightly. Click [Save]. When The King Group - QuickBooks Accountant 2014 appears, the file is restored.
7. Continue with the next section "My Company."

My Company

Before recording transactions for The King Group, look at the My Company information included on the Problem 06.2A.The King Group.QBM file.

1. From the Icon Bar, select [My Company]. (*Or,* from the menu bar, select Company; My Company.) The My Company window appears.

2. To add your name to the Company Name field, click [ ]. Close the My Company window.

The King Group Trial Balance

Display or print the December 31, 2016 trial balance. Compare your trial balance with the one shown on the next page.

The King Group
Trial Balance
As of December 31, 2016

	Dec 31, 16	
	Debit	Credit
101 · Cash	93,400.00	
111 · Accounts Receivable	13,000.00	
121 · Supplies	8,000.00	
131 · Prepaid Advertising	32,000.00	
141 · Equipment	85,000.00	
202 · Accounts Payable		13,000.00
301 · Delva King, Capital		142,000.00
302 · Delva King, Drawing	9,400.00	
401 · Fees Income		103,500.00
511 · Salaries Expense	15,400.00	
514 · Utilities Expense	2,300.00	
TOTAL	258,500.00	258,500.00

Required:

1. Journalize and post the adjusting entries shown below. Date the adjusting entries 12/31/2016. (*Hint:* On the Make General Journal Entries window, put a check mark in the Adjusting Entry box.)

The King Group
Partial Worksheet
Month Ended, December 31, 2016

Account Name	Trial Balance		Adjustments	
	Debit	Credit	Debit	Credit
Supplies	8,000.00			(a)3,400.00
Prepaid Advertising	32,000.00			(b)4,000.00
Accumulated Depreciation-Equipment				(c)3,400.00
Supplies Expense			(a)3,400.00	
Advertising Expense			(b)4,000.00	
Depreciation Expense-Equipment			(c)3,400.00	

2. Print the 12/31/2016 Adjusting Journal Entries. (Report Center *or* Reports menu; Accountant & Taxes, Adjusting Journal Entries.)
3. Print the 12/31/2016 Adjusted Trial Balance. (Report Center *or* Reports menu; Accountant & Taxes, Adjusted Trial Balance.)
4. Back up. The suggested file name is **Problem 06.2A.Adjusted.QBM.**

---

5. Journalize and post the closing entries. Date the closing entries 12/31/2016. (*Hint:* On the Make General Journal Entries window, uncheck Adjusting Entry.)
6. Print the 12/31/2016 journal. (*Hint:* Adjusting Entries have a checkmark in the Adj. column.)
7. Print the 12/1/2016 to 12/31/2016 General Ledger.
8. Print the 12/1/2016 to 12/31/2016 postclosing trial balance.
9. Back up. The suggested file name is **Problem 06.2A.Closed.QBM**.
10. **Analyze:** How many accounts are listed in the Adjusted Trial Balance? How many accounts are listed on the postclosing trial balance? Use a blank piece of paper or the *Working Paper*s to answer the analysis question.

MINI-PRACTICE SET 1: SERVICE BUSINESS ACCOUNTING CYCLE

This project will give you an opportunity to apply your knowledge of accounting principles and procedures by handling all the accounts of Wells' Consulting Services for the month of January 2017.

Assume that you are the chief accountant for Wells' Consulting Services. During January, the business will use the same types of records and procedures that you learned about in the textbook's Chapters 1-6.

Follow the steps below to restore the Mini Practice Set 1.Wells' Consulting Services.QBM file.

Instructions:

1. Start QuickBooks.
2. If the menu bar shows a company name, click File; Open or Restore Company.
3. The Open or Restore Company window appears. Select Restore a portable file.
4. Click [Next]. The Open Portable Company File window appears. In the Look in field, go to the appropriate location for the Mini Practice Set 1.Wells' Consulting Services.QBM file. Click on the file to highlight it. Click [Open]. (*Hint:* You can also double-click on the file name.)
5. The Open or Restore Company window appears. Click [Next].
6. The Save Company File as window appears. Accept the default file name or change it slightly. Click [Save]. When Wells' Consulting Services - QuickBooks Accountant 2014 appears, the file is restored. Continue with the next section "My Company."

My Company

Before recording transactions for Wells' Consulting Services, look at the My Company information included on the Mini Practice Set 1.Wells' Consulting Services.QBM file.

1. From the Icon Bar, select **My Company**. (*Or,* from the menu bar, select Company; My Company.) The My Company window appears.

2. To add your name to the Company Name field, click [pencil icon]. Close the My Company window.

Wells' Consulting Services' Chart of Accounts

The chart of accounts for Wells' Consulting Services has been expanded to include a few new accounts. Print or display the chart of accounts and compare it to the one below.

Assets	Revenue
101 Cash	401 Fees Income
111 Accounts Receivable	**Expenses**
121 Supplies	511 Salaries Expense
134 Prepaid Insurance	514 Utilities Expense
137 Prepaid Rent	517 Supplies Expense
141 Equipment	520 Rent Expense
142 Accumulated Depreciation-Equipment	523 Depreciation Expense-Equipment
Liabilities	526 Advertising Expense
202 Accounts Payable	529 Maintenance Expense
Owner's Equity	532 Telephone Expense
301 Carolyn Wells, Capital	535 Insurance Expense
302 Carolyn Wells, Drawing	
309 Income Summary	

January 1, 2017 Trial Balance

Print or display the January 1, 2017 trial balance. The account balances agree with the December 31, 2016 postclosing trial balance shown in the textbook page 166, Figure 6.3. These are also the beginning account balances shown in the general ledger accounts as of January 1, 2017.

Wells' Consulting Services
Trial Balance
As of January 1, 2017

	Jan 1, 17	
	Debit	Credit
101 · Cash	▶ 111,350.00 ◀	
111 · Accounts Receivable	5,000.00	
121 · Supplies	1,000.00	
137 · Prepaid Rent	4,000.00	
141 · Equipment	11,000.00	
142 · Accumulated Deprec.-Equipment		183.00
202 · Accounts Payable		3,500.00
300 · Opening Balance Equity	0.00	
301 · Carolyn Wells, Capital		128,667.00
TOTAL	132,350.00	132,350.00

January 2017 Transactions

The transactions for Wells' Consulting Services are shown below and on page 33. Read the required steps on pages 33-34 to complete the Mini-Practice Set 1. Three backups are suggested—1) Mini Practice Set 1.January.QBM; 2) Mini Practice Set 1.Adjusted.QBM; and 3) Mini Practice Set 1.Closed.QBM.

Date	Transactions

Jan. 2 Purchased supplies for $6,000; issued Check 1015.

2 Purchased a one-year insurance policy for $7,200; issued Check 1016.

7 Sold services for $20,000 in cash and $4,000 on credit during the first week of January.

12 Collected a total of $4,000 on account from credit customers during the first week of January.

12 Issued Check 1017 for $3,200 to pay for special promotional advertising to new businesses on the local radio station during the month.

13 Collected a total of $3,500 on account from credit customers during the second week of January.

14 Returned supplies that were damaged for a cash refund of $650.

15 Sold services for $20,700 in cash and $2,300 on credit during the second week of January.

20 Purchased supplies for $4,600 from White's, Inc.; received Invoice 2384 payable in 30 days.

20 Sold services for $12,500 in cash and $3,350 on credit during the third week of January.

20 Collected a total of $4,500 on account from credit customers during the third week of January.

21 Issued Check 1018 for $6,075 to pay for maintenance work on the office equipment

22 Issued Check 1019 for $3,200 to pay for special promotional advertising to new businesses in the local newspaper.

23 Received the monthly telephone bill for $925 and paid it with Check 1020.

26 Collected a total of $1,600 on account from credit customers during the fourth week of January.

27 Issued Check 1021 for $3,000 to Office Plus, as payment on account for Invoice 2223.

28 Sent Check 1022 for $2,350 in payment of the monthly bill for utilities.

29 Sold services for $19,000 in cash and $2,750 on credit during the fourth week of January.

31 Issued Checks 1023–1027 for $25,750 to pay the monthly salaries of the regular employees and three part-time workers.

31 Issued Check 1028 for $15,000 for personal use.

31 Issued Check 1029 for $4,150 to pay for maintenance services for the month.

31 Purchased additional equipment for $15,000 from Contemporary Equipment Company; issued Check 1030 for $10,000 and bought the rest on credit. The equipment has a five-year life and no salvage value.

31 Sold services for $5,600 in cash and $1,580 on credit on January 31.

Required:

1. Journalize and post each transaction and record it in the general journal. The transactions are shown on pages 32-33.
2. Print the 1/1/2017 to 1/31/2017 unadjusted trial balance.
3. Backup. The suggested file name is **Mini Practice Set 1.January.QBM**.
4. Journalize and post the following adjusting entries. Date the adjustments January 31, 2017 as the date. (*Hint:* On he Make General Journal Entries window, put a checkmark in the Adjusting Entry field.)
   a. Journalize and post the adjustment for supplies used during the month. An inventory taken on January 31 showed supplies of $4,200 on hand.
   b. Compute, then journalize and post the adjustment for expired insurance for the month.
   c. Journalize and post the adjustment for one month of expired rent of $4,000.

     d. Journalize and post the adjustment for depreciation of $183 on the old equipment for the month. The first adjustment for depreciation for the new equipment will be recorded in February.

5. Print the adjusted trial balance.
6. Print the profit & loss report. (Substitute the P&L for the textbook's income statement.)
7. Print the balance sheet. (Substitute the equity section for the statement of owner's equity.)
8. Backup. The suggested file name is **Mini Practice Set 1.Adjusted.QBM**.
9. Journalize and post the closing entries.
10. Print the January 2-31, 2017 journal report.
11. Print the January 1-31, 2017 general ledger.
12. Print the postclosing trial balance.
13. Backup. The suggested file name is **Mini Practice Set 1.Closed.QBM**.
14. **Analyze:** Compare the January 31 balance sheet you prepared with the December 31 balance sheet shown in the textbook on page 167.
     a. What changes occurred in total assets, liabilities, and the owner's ending capital?
     b. What changes occurred in Cash and Accounts Receivable accounts?
     c. Has there been an improvement in the firm's financial position? Why or why not?

Chapter 7

Accounting for Sales and Accounts Receivable

In Chapter 7 of *College Accounting, 14e,* there are three QuickBooks problems.

➢ Problem 7.1A Best Appliances: Recording credit sales and posting from the sales journal.
➢ Problem 7.2A Towncenter Furniture: Journalizing, posting, and reporting sales transactions.
➢ Problem 7.4A Bella Floral Designs: Recording sales transactions, posting to the accounts receivable ledger, and preparing a schedule of accounts receivable.

Chapter 7's QuickBooks activities demonstrate how to:

* Restore three QuickBooks problem templates.
* Journalize and post transactions.
* Print the journal.
* Print the general ledger and customer ledgers.
* Complete Problem 7.1A, Problem 7.2A, and Problem 7.4A.

GETTING STARTED: Problem 7.1A

Use the following steps to start QuickBooks and restore the Problem 07.1A.Best Appliances.QBM file.

Instructions:

1. Start QuickBooks.
2. If the menu bar shows a company name, click File; Open or Restore Company.
3. The Open or Restore Company window appears. Select Restore a portable file.
4. Click 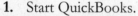 . The Open Portable Company File window appears. In the Look in field, go to the appropriate location for the Problem 07.1A.Best

   Appliances.QBM file. Click on the file to highlight it. Click Open . (*Hint:* You can also double-click on the file name.)
5. The Open or Restore Company window appears. Click Next .
6. The Save Company File as window appears. Accept the default file name or change it

   slightly. Click Save . When Best Appliances - QuickBooks Accountant 2014 appears, the file is restored.

My Company

Before recording transactions for Best Appliances, look at the My Company information included on the Problem 07.1A.Best Appliances.QBM file.

1. From the Icon Bar, select 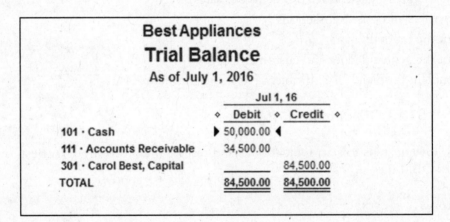 . (*Or*, from the menu bar, select Company; My Company.) The My Company window appears.

2. To add your name to the Company Name field, click [pencil icon]. Close the My Company window.

Best Appliances Trial Balance

Best Appliances is a retail store that sells household appliances. The trial balance below shows that Account No. 111, Accounts Receivable has a balance of $34,500. The balance shown for accounts receivable is for the beginning of the month. Display the July 1, 2016 trial balance.

Best Appliances
Trial Balance
As of July 1, 2016

	Jul 1, 16	
	Debit	Credit
101 · Cash	▶ 50,000.00 ◀	
111 · Accounts Receivable	34,500.00	
301 · Carol Best, Capital		84,500.00
TOTAL	84,500.00	84,500.00

Journalizing and Posting Sales

In QuickBooks, use the Customers Create Invoices selections for credit sales. Merchandise sales are subject to an 8 percent sales tax. Detailed steps for journalizing and posting the July 1 transaction are shown after the transactions. Follow the instructions on pages 37-38 to record the July 1 transaction.

July 1   Sold a dishwasher to Perry Martin; issued Sales Slip 501 for $1,150 plus sales tax of $92. (Detailed steps for completing the July 1 transaction are shown on the next page.)

6   Sold a washer to Cindy Han; issued Sales Slip 502 for $2,425 plus sales tax of $194.

11 Sold a high-definition television set to Richard Slocomb; issued Sales Slip 503 for $2,600 plus sales tax of $208.

17 Sold an electric dryer to Mary Schneider; issued Sales Slip 504 for $1,275 plus sales tax of $102.

23 Sold a trash compactor to Veronica Velazquez; issued Sales Slip 505 for $900 plus sales tax of $72.

27 Sold a color television set to Jeff Budd; issued Sales Slip 506 for $1,725 plus sales tax of $138.

29 Sold an electric range to Michelle Ly; issued Sales Slip 507 for $1,450 plus sales tax of $116.

31 Sold a double oven to Phil Long; issued Sales Slip 508 for $625 plus sales tax of $50.

Credit Sales: Create Invoice

Date   *Transaction*

July 1   Sold a dishwasher to Perry Martin; issued Sales Slip 501 for $1,150 plus sales tax of $92.

1. Go to QuickBooks' Home page. (*Hint:* If necessary, click  on the Icon Bar.)

2. In the Customers area, click ⬚ Create Invoices. The Create Invoices window appears.
3. In the Customer:Job field, select 15Martin, for Perry Martin. Observe that the Bill To field is automatically completed.
4. Type **7/1/2016** in the Date field. Press <Tab>.
5. Type **501** in the Invoice # field. Press <Tab>.
6. Go to the Item Code field. Select Dishwasher.
7. Type **1,150** in the Price Each field. Observe that 1,150.00 automatically appears in the Amount field.
8. In the Item Code field, select Sales Tax.
9. Type **92** in the Price Each field.
10. Uncheck the Print Later box. Compare your Create Invoices window to the one shown on the next page.

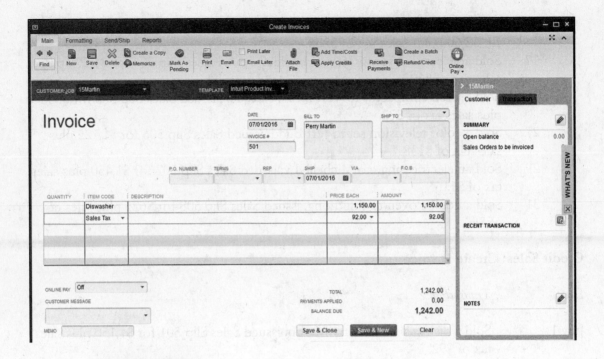

11. Click **Save & New**. The Create Invoices window is ready for the next transaction. Record July 6-31 transactions shown on page 36-37.

QB Journal Transactions

QuickBooks' Journal shows how each transaction was debited and credited. Follow these steps to see the July 1 through 31, 2016 transactions.

1. Select the Report Center or Reports menu; Accountant & Taxes, Journal.
2. Type **7/1/2016** in the From field.
3. Type **7/31/2016** in the To field. The journal entries display.
4. Make the selections to display or print.

Required:

1. Journalize and post the July 1-31, 2016 transactions.
2. Print the 7/1/2016 to 7/31/2016 journal report.
3. Print the 7/1/2016 to 7/31/2016 general ledger.
4. Back up. The suggested file name is **Problem 07.1A.QBM**.
5. **Analyze:** What percentage of credit sales were for entertainment items? (*Hint:* From the menu bar, select Reports; Sales, Sales by Item Summary.) Use a blank piece of paper or the *Working Papers* to complete the analysis question.

GETTING STARTED: Problem 7.2A

Follow the steps below to restore the Problem 07.2A.Towncenter Furniture.QBM file.

Instructions:

1. Start QuickBooks.
2. If the menu bar shows a company name, click File; Open or Restore Company.
3. The Open or Restore Company window appears. Select Restore a portable file.
4. Click [Next]. The Open Portable Company File window appears. In the Look in field, go to the appropriate location for the Problem 07.2A.Towncenter Furniture.QBM file. Click on the file to highlight it. Click [Open]. (*Hint:* You can also double-click on the file name.)
5. The Open or Restore Company window appears. Click [Next].
6. The Save Company File as window appears. Accept the default file name or change it slightly. Click [Save]. When Towncenter Furniture - QuickBooks Accountant 2014 appears, the file is restored.
7. Continue with the next section "My Company."

My Company

Before recording transactions for Towncenter Furniture, look at the My Company information included on the Problem 07.2A.Towncenter Furniture.QBM file.

1. From the Icon Bar, select [My Company]. (*Or,* from the menu bar, select Company; My Company.) The My Company window appears.

2. To add your name to the Company Name field, click [✏️]. Close the My Company window.

Towncenter Furniture Trial Balance

Towncenter Furniture specializes in modern living room and dining room furniture. Merchandise sales are subject to an 8 percent sales tax. The firm's credit sales and sales returns and allowances for February 2016 are reflected in the transactions shown below and on the next page.

Before you record the February 1-28 transactions, display or print the February 1, 2016 trial balance.

```
              Towncenter Furniture
                  Trial Balance
               As of February 1, 2016

                                    Feb 1, 16
                              ◇  Debit  ◇  Credit  ◇
101 · Cash                  ▶ 15,634.00 ◀
111 · Accounts Receivable     16,636.00
231 · Sales Tax Payable                      7,270.00
301 · Matt Reva, Capital                    25,000.00
TOTAL                         32,270.00     32,270.00
```

Instructions:

1. Journalize and post the February 1 through 9 sales transactions.
2. Follow the steps on pages 41-42 to journalize and post the February 11 sales return.

Feb. 1   Sold a living room sofa to Sun Yoo; issued Sales Slip 1615 for $4,790 plus sales tax of $383.20.

5   Sold three recliners to Jacqueline Moore; issued Sales Slip 1616 for $2,350 plus sales tax of $188.

9   Sold a dining room set to Hazel Tran; issued Sales Slip 1617 for $6,550 plus sales tax of $524.

11   Accepted a return of one damaged recliner from Jacqueline Moore that was originally sold on Sales Slip 1616 of February 5; issued Credit Memorandum 702 for $1,026, which includes sales tax of $76. (Detailed steps for recording this transaction are shown on pages 41-42.) In QB, sales returns are debited to Account No. 401 Sales; Account No. 111 Accounts Receivable/customer account is credited.

17   Sold living room tables and bookcases to Ann Brown; issued Sales Slip 1618 for $9,550 plus sales tax of $764.

23   Sold eight dining room chairs to Domingo Salas; issued Sales Slip 1619 for $3,650 plus sales tax of $292.

25   Gave Ann Brown an allowance for scratches on her bookcases; issued Credit Memorandum 703 for $702, which includes sales taxes of $52; the bookcases were originally sold on Sales Slip 1618 of February 17.

27   Sold a living room sofa and four chairs to Jose Saucedo; issued Sales Slip 1620 for $4,225 plus sales tax of $338.

28   Sold a dining room table to Mimi Yuki; issued Sales Slip 1621 for $2,050 plus sales tax of $164.

28   Sold a living room modular wall unit to Alan Baker; issued Sales Slip 1622 for $3,900 plus sales tax of $312.

Sales Returns

In QuickBooks, when a customer returns merchandise use the Refunds & Credits selection.

Date	Transaction
Feb. 11	Accepted a return of one damaged recliner from Jacqueline Moore that was originally sold on Sales Slip 1616 of February 5; issued Credit Memorandum 702 for $1,206.00, which includes sales tax of $76.00.

1. If necessary, go to the Home page. In the Customer area, select _____ . The Create Credit Memos/Refunds window appears.
2. In the Customer:Job field, select 14Moore, for the customer Jacqueline Moore.
3. Type or select **2/11/2016** as the <u>D</u>ate.
4. Type **CM702** in the Credit No. field.
5. In the Item field, select Recliner.
6. Type **1** in the Qty field.
7. Type **950** in the Rate field.
8. In the Item field, select Sales Tax.
9. Type **76** in the Rate field.
10. Uncheck the Print Later box. Compare your Create Credit Memos/Refunds window with the one shown below.

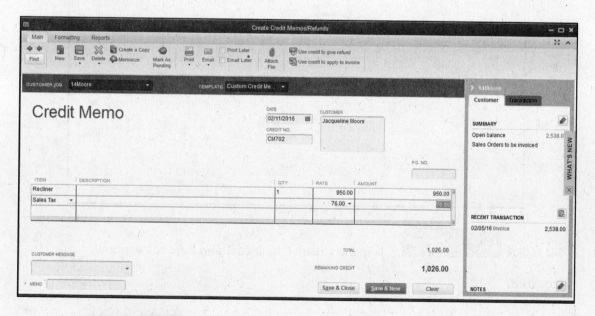

11. Click [Save & New] .

---

12. When the Available Credit window appears, select Apply to an invoice.

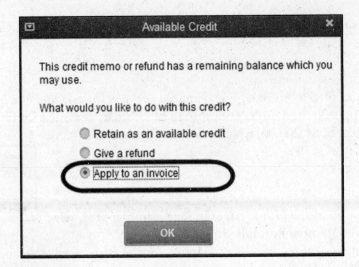

13. Click [OK]. The Apply Credit to Invoices window appears showing the appropriate Invoice Number, 1616.

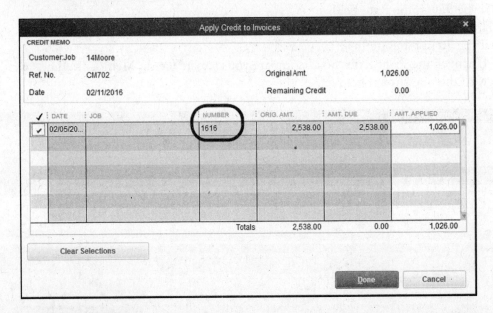

14. Click [Done]. Close the Create Credit Memos/Refunds window.

Required:

1. Journalize and post the February 17-28, 2016 transactions. (*Hint:* For the February 17 sales invoice, type the Sales Slip No. in the Invoice # field.)

---

2. Print the February 1-28, 2016 journal. In QuickBooks, sales returns are debited to Account No. 401, Sales (CM702 and CM703).
3. Print the general ledger. (QB sales account balance includes sales returns. QB does *not* post sales returns to a separate sales returns and allowances account.)
4. Print the income statement. (QB P&L report does not show sales returns and allowances.)
5. Back up. The suggested file name is **Problem 07.2A.QBM**.
6. **Analyze:** Based on the beginning balance of the Sales Tax Payable account, what was the amount of net sales for January? (*Hint:* Sales tax returns are filed and paid to the state quarterly.) Use a blank piece of paper or the *Working Papers* to complete the analysis question.

GETTING STARTED: Problem 7.4A

Follow the steps below to restore the Problem 07.4A Bella Floral Designs.QBM file.

Instructions:

1. Start QuickBooks.
2. If the menu bar shows a company name, click File; Open or Restore Company.
3. The Open or Restore Company window appears. Select Restore a portable file.
4. Click **Next** . The Open Portable Company File window appears. In the Look in field, go to the appropriate location for the Problem 07.4A.Bella Floral Designs.QBM file. Click on the file to highlight it. Click **Open** . (*Hint:* You can also double-click on the file name.)
5. The Open or Restore Company window appears. Click **Next** .
6. The Save Company File as window appears. Accept the default file name or change it slightly. Click **Save** . When Bella Floral Designs - QuickBooks Accountant 2014 appears, the file is restored.
7. Continue with the next section "My Company."

My Company

Before recording transactions for Bella Floral Designs, look at the My Company information included on the Problem 07.4A.Bella Floral Designs.QBM file.

1. From the Icon Bar, select **My Company**. (*Or,* from the menu bar, select Company; My Company.) The My Company window appears.

2. To add your name to the Company Name field, click .

Bella Floral Designs is a wholesale shop that sells flowers, plants, and plant supplies. The transactions below took place during January 2016.

Required:

1. Journalize and post the January 3 through 31, 2016 sales transactions.

Jan. 3   Sold a floral arrangement to Thomas Florist; issued Invoice 1081 for $600.

     8   Sold potted plants to Carter Garden Supply; issued Invoice 1082 for $825.

     9   Sold floral arrangements to Thomasville Flower Shop; issued Invoice 1083 for $482.

    10   Sold corsages to Moore's Flower Shop; issued Invoice 1084 for $630.

    15   Gave Thomasville Flower Shop an allowance because of withered blossoms discovered in one of the floral arrangements sold on Invoice 1083 on January 9; issued Credit Memorandum 101 for $60.

    20   Sold table arrangements to Cedar Hill Floral Shop; issued Invoice 1085 for $580.

    22   Sold plants to Applegate Nursery; issued Invoice 1086 for $780.

    25   Sold roses to Moore's Flower Shop; issued Invoice 1087 for $437. (*Hint:* Select plants as the item.)

    27   Sold several floral arrangements to Thomas Florist; issued Invoice 1088 for $975.

    31   Gave Thomas Florist an allowance because of withered blossoms discovered in one of the floral arrangements sold on Invoice 1088 on January 27; issued Credit Memorandum 102 for $200. (When the Available Credit window appears, select Apply to an invoice. Then, apply this credit to Invoice No. 1088.)

2. Print the January 3-31, 2016 journal. In QuickBooks, sales returns are debited to Account No. 401, Sales (CM101 and CM102.)
3. Print the January 1-31, 2016 general ledger. (QB sales account includes sales returns. QB does *not* post sales returns to a separate sales returns and allowances account.)
4. Print the January 1-31, 2016 Customer Balance Detail report. (Reports or Report Center; Customers & Receivables, Customer Balance Detail). QB Customer Balance Detail report includes each customer's balance and a total. Substitute Customer Balance Detail report for the accounts receivable subsidiary ledger,
5. Back up. The suggested file name is **Problem 07.4A.QBM**.
6. **Analyze:** Damaged goods decreased sales by what dollar amount? By what percentage amount? Use a blank piece of paper or the *Working Papers* to complete the analysis question.

Chapter 8

Accounting for Purchases and Accounts Payable

In Chapter 8 of *College Accounting, 14e,* there are three QuickBooks problems.

➢ Problem 8.1A Digital World: Journalizing credit purchases and purchases returns and allowances and posting to the general ledger.

➢ Problem 8.3A The English Garden Shop: Journalizing credit purchases and purchases returns and allowances, computing the net delivered cost of goods, posting to the general ledger, posting to the accounts payable ledger, and preparing a schedule of accounts payable.

➢ Problem 8.4A Office Plus: Journalizing credit purchases and purchases returns and allowances, posting to the general ledger, posting to the accounts payable ledger, and preparing a schedule of accounts payable.

Chapter 8's QuickBooks activities demonstrate how to:

• Restore three QuickBooks problem templates.
• Journalize and post accounts payable transactions.
• Print the journal.
• Print the vendor balance detail report.
• Complete Problem 8.1A, Problem 8.3A, and Problem 8.4A.

GETTING STARTED: Problem 8.1A

1. Start QuickBooks.
2. If the menu bar shows a company name, click File; Open or Restore Company.
3. The Open or Restore Company window appears. Select Restore a portable file.

4. Click **Next**. The Open Portable Company File window appears. In the Look in field, go to the appropriate location for the Problem 08.1A.Digital World.QBM file. Click on the file to highlight it. Click **Open**. (*Hint:* You can also double-click on the file name.)

5. The Open or Restore Company window appears. Click **Next**.
6. The Save Company File as window appears. Accept the default file name or change it slightly. Click **Save**. When Digital World - QuickBooks Accountant 2014 appears, the file is restored.
7. Continue with the next section "My Company."

My Company

Before recording transactions for Digital World, look at the My Company information included on the Problem 08.1A.Digital World.QBM file.

1. From the Icon Bar, select 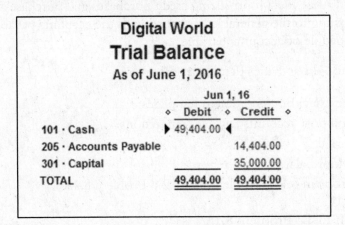 My Company. (*Or*, from the menu bar, select Company; My Company.) The My Company window appears.

2. To add your name to the Company Name field, click ✏. Close the My Company window.

Display the Trial Balance

Display the June 1, 2016 trial balance. The trial balance below shows that Account No. 205, Accounts Payable has a balance of $14,404.

Digital World
Trial Balance
As of June 1, 2016

	Jun 1, 16	
	Debit	Credit
101 · Cash	49,404.00	
205 · Accounts Payable		14,404.00
301 · Capital		35,000.00
TOTAL	49,404.00	49,404.00

Journalizing Credit Purchases and Purchases Returns and Allowances

Digital World is a retail store that sells cameras and photography supplies. The firm's credit purchases and purchases returns and allowances transactions for June 2016 appear below and on page 47. The general ledger accounts needed to record these transactions are included on the Problem 08.1A.Digital World.QBM file.

Detailed steps for completing the June 1 credit purchase and the June 18 purchase return are shown on pages 47-48.

Date	Transactions
June 1	Purchased instant cameras for $2,050 plus a freight charge of $230 from Pro Photo Equipment, Invoice 4241, dated May 27; the terms are 60 days net.
8	Purchased film for $1,394 from Photo Supplies, Invoice 1102, dated June 3, net payable in 45 days.

12	Purchased lenses for $916 from Nano Glass, Invoice 7282, dated June 9; the terms are 1/10, n/60.
18	Received Credit Memorandum 110 for $400 from Pro Photo Equipment for defective cameras that were returned; they were originally purchased on Invoice 4241, dated May 27.
20	Purchased color film for $1,200 plus freight of $75 from Photo Supplies, Invoice 1148, dated June 15, net payable in 45 days.
23	Purchased camera cases for $1,956 from Hi-Qual Case, Invoice 3108, dated June 18, net due and payable in 45 days.
28	Purchased lens filters for $2,470 plus freight of $120 from Holtz Spectrum, Invoice 5027, dated June 24; the terms are 2/10, n/30.
30	Received Credit Memorandum 1108 for $310 from Hi-Qual Case; the amount is an allowance for damaged but usable goods purchased on Invoice 3108, dated June 18.

Credit Purchases: Follow these steps to complete the June 1 transaction.

Date   *Transaction*

June 1   Purchased instant cameras for $2,050 plus a freight charge of $230 from Pro Photo Equipment, Invoice 4241, dated May 27; the terms are 60 days net.

Instructions:

1. Go to QuickBooks' Home page. (*Hint:* If necessary, click **🏠 Home** .)

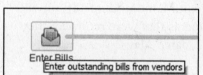

2. In the Vendors area, click . The Enter Bills window appears.
3. In the Vendor field, select 59Pro Photo (Pro Photo Equipment).
4. Type **6/1/2016** as the date.
5. Type **4241** in the Ref. No. field. (*Hint:* In the Ref. No. field, use the Invoice number.)
6. Type **2280** in the Amount Due field. (*Hint:* The purchase amount of $2,050 plus the freight charge of $230: 2,050+230=2,280.)
7. In the Account field, 501 Purchases is shown. Type **2050** as the amount. (*Hint:* Change the default amount of 2280 to 2050.)
8. In the Account field, select Account No. 502 Freight In to debit that account. Observe that 230.00 is automatically shown in the Amount field. The Bill Due field is also automatically completed. Compare your Enter Bills window to the one shown on the next page.

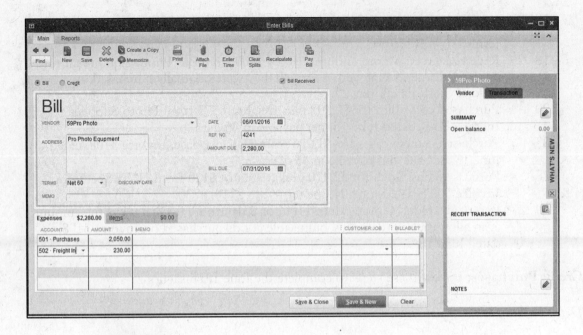

10. Click ![Save & New]. The Enter Bills window is ready for the next transaction. Journalize and post the June 8 and 12 transactions shown on pages 46-47.

Purchase Returns: Follow the steps below to return merchandise to a vendor.

Date   *Transaction*

June 18   Received Credit Memorandum 110 for $400 from Pro Photo Equipment for defective cameras that were returned; they were originally purchased on Invoice 4241, dated May 27.

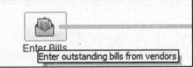

1. If necessary, in the Vendors area, click ![Enter Bills]. The Enter Bills window appears.
2. Click on the radio button next to Credit.
3. Select the vendor, Pro Photo Equipment.
4. Type **6/18/2016** or select the date.
5. Type **CM110** in the Ref. No. field.
6. Type **400** in the Credit Amount field.
7. In the Account field, select Account No. 503, Purchases Returns and Allowances. The Amount field is automatically completed.

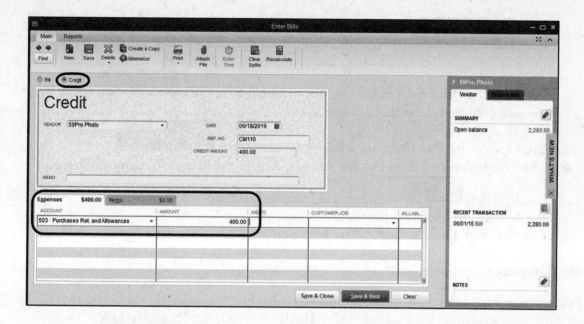

8. Click **Save & Close**. You are returned to the Home page. Continue journalizing and posting the June 20 through June 30 transactions.

Required:

1. Journalize and post the June 20-30 transactions. (*Hint:* For the June 20 and June 28 transactions, debit Account No. 501 Purchases *and* Account No. 502 Freight for the appropriate amounts.)
2. Print the June 1-30, 2016 journal.
3. Print the June 1-30, 2016 general ledger.
4. Use a blank piece of paper or the *Working Papers* to compute net purchases of the firm for the month of June.
5. Back up. The suggested file name is **Problem 08.1A.QBM**
6. **Analyze:** What total purchases were posted to the Purchases general ledger account for June? Use a blank piece of paper or the *Working Papers* to answer the analysis question.

GETTING STARTED: Problem 8.3A

Use the following steps to start QuickBooks and restore the Problem 08.3A.The English Garden Shop.QBM file.

Instructions:

1. Start QuickBooks.
2. If the menu bar shows a company name, click File; Open or Restore Company.
3. The Open or Restore Company window appears. Select Restore a portable file.

---

4. Click **Next**. The Open Portable Company File window appears. In the Look in field, go to the appropriate location for the Problem 08.3A.The English Garden Shop.QBM file. Click on the file to highlight it. Click **Open**. (*Hint:* You can also double-click on the file name.)

5. The Open or Restore Company window appears. Click **Next**.

6. The Save Company File as window appears. Accept the default file name or change it slightly. Click **Save**. When The English Garden Shop - QuickBooks Accountant 2014 appears, the file is restored.

7. Continue with the next section "My Company."

My Company

Before recording transactions for The English Garden Shop, look at the My Company information included on the Problem 08.3A.The English Garden Shop.QBM file.

1. From the Icon Bar, select **My Company**. (*Or,* from the menu bar, select Company; My Company.) The My Company window appears.

2. To add your name to the Company Name field, click [pencil icon]. Close the My Company window.

Displaying the Vendor Ledgers and the Accounts Payable Balance

The English Garden Shop is a retail store that sells garden equipment, furniture, and supplies. Its credit purchases and purchases returns and allowances for July are shown on pages 51-52. The general ledger accounts used to record these transactions are on the Problem 08.3A.The English Garden Shop.QBM file.

The QuickBooks file for Problem 8.3A includes vendor account balances. Follow these steps to display the vendor ledgers.

1. Go to the Reports menu or the Report Center; Vendors & Payables, Vendor Balance Detail.

2. Type **7/1/2016** to **7/1/2016** in the From the To fields, respectively. Click **Refresh**. The July 1, 2016 Vendor Balance Detail report appears.

The English Garden Shop
Vendor Balance Detail
As of July 1, 2016

Type	Date	Num	Account	Amount	Balance
111Brooks					**11,220.00**
Total 111Brooks					11,220.00 ◄
112Brown					**18,220.00**
Total 112Brown					18,220.00
114Lawn					**6,540.00**
Total 114Lawn					6,540.00
TOTAL					**35,980.00**

3. Observe that the vendor balances total 35,980.00. This is the balance in Account No. 205, Accounts Payable. To see the accounts payable balance, display the general ledger report. Follow these steps to view the accounts payable balance.

   a. Go to the Reports menu or the Report Center; select Accountant & Taxes, General Ledger.
   b. Type **7/1/2016** to **7/1/2016** in the From and To fields, respectively. Observe that Account No. 205, Accounts Payable shows a balance of $35,980.00. Account No. 205, Accounts Payable is shown below.

205 · Accounts Payable	-35,980.00
Total 205 · Accounts Payable	-35,980.00

   c. Close the reports without saving.

Required:

1. Journalize and post the July 1 – 31, 2016 transactions.

   July 1   Purchased lawn mowers for $9,310 plus a freight charge of $259 from Brown Corporation, Invoice 1011, dated June 26, net due and payable in 60 days.
   5   Purchased outdoor chairs and tables for $4,470 plus a freight charge of $562 from Brooks Garden Furniture Company, Invoice 639, dated July 2, net due and payable in 45 days.
   9   Purchased grass seed for $1,590 from Lawn and Gardens Supply, Invoice 8164, dated July 5; the terms are 30 days net.
   16   Received Credit Memorandum 110 for $700 from Brooks Garden Furniture Company; the amount is an allowance for scratches on some of the chairs and tables originally purchased on Invoice 639, dated July 2.
   19   Purchased fertilizer for $1,300 plus a freight charge of $266 from Lawn and Gardens Supply, Invoice 9050, dated July 15; the terms are 30 days net.

21 Purchased hoses from Cameron Rubber Company for $3,780 plus a freight charge of $234, Invoice 1785, dated July 17; terms are 1/15, n/60.

28 Received Credit Memorandum 223 for $530 from Cameron Rubber Company for damaged hoses that were returned; the goods were purchased on Invoice 1785, dated July 17.

31 Purchased lawn sprinkler systems for $10,410 plus a freight charge of $288 from Wilson Industrial Products, Invoice 8985, dated July 26; the terms are 2/10, n/30.

2. Print the July 1-31, 2016 journal.
3. Print the July 1-31, 2016 general ledger.
4. Print the Vendor Balance Detail report. (*Hint:* Substitute QuickBooks' vendor detail report for the accounts payable subsidiary ledger and schedule of accounts payable.)
5. Check the total of the Vendor Balance Detail report against the balance of the Accounts Payable account in the general ledger. The two amounts should be the same.
6. Back up. The suggested file name is **Problem 08.3A.QBM**.
7. Use a blank piece of paper or the *Working Papers* to compute the net delivered cost of the firm's purchases for the month of July.
8. **Analyze:** What total freight charges were posted to the general ledger for the month of July? Use a blank piece of paper or the *Working Papers* to answer the analysis question.

GETTING STARTED: Problem 8.4A

Use the following steps to start QuickBooks and restore the Problem 08.4A.Office Plus.QBM file.

Instructions:

1. Start QuickBooks.
2. If the menu bar shows a company name, click File; Open or Restore Company.
3. The Open or Restore Company window appears. Select Restore a portable file.
4. Click [Next]. The Open Portable Company File window appears. In the Look in field, go to the appropriate location for the Problem 08.4A.Office Plus.QBM file. Click on the file to highlight it. Click [Open]. (*Hint:* You can also double-click on the file name.)
5. The Open or Restore Company window appears. Click [Next].
6. The Save Company File as window appears. Accept the default file name or change it slightly. Click [Save]. When Office Plus - QuickBooks Accountant 2014 appears, the file is restored.
7. Continue with the next section "My Company."

My Company

Before recording transactions for the Office Plus, look at the My Company information included on the Problem 08.4A.Office Plus.QBM file.

1. From the Icon Bar, select [My Company]. (*Or*, from the menu bar, select Company; My Company.) The My Company window appears.

2. To add your name to the Company Name field, click [pencil icon]. Close the My Company window.

Displaying the Vendor Ledgers and Accounts Payable Balance

Office Plus is a retail business that sells office equipment, furniture, and supplies. Its credit purchases and purchases returns and allowances for September 2016 are shown on page 54.

The Problem 08.4A.Office Plus.QBM file includes vendor balances, which agrees with the general ledger's accounts payable balance.

1. Display the September 1, 2016 Vendor Balance Detail report and general ledger. Observe that the vendor ledgers report total equals the ending balance in accounts payable.

Office Plus
Vendor Balance Detail
As of September 1, 2016

Type	Date	Num	Account	Amount	Balance
111Apex					**11,060.00**
Total 111Apex					11,060.00 ◀
112Brown					**2,220.00**
Total 112Brown					2,220.00
113Dalton					**9,676.00**
Total 113Dalton					9,676.00
115Zenn					**5,400.00**
Total 115Zenn					5,400.00
TOTAL					**28,356.00**

205 · Accounts Payable	-28,356.00
Total 205 · Accounts Payable	-28,356.00

2. Close the reports.

Required:

1. Journalize and post the September 3–30, 2016 transactions.

Sept. 3 Purchased desks for $8,020 plus a freight charge of $222 from Dalton Office Furniture Company, Invoice 4213, dated August 29; the terms are 30 days net.

  7 Purchased computers for $12,300 from Apex Office Machines, Inc., Invoice 9217, dated September 2, net due and payable in 60 days.

 10 Received Credit Memorandum 511 for $700 from Dalton Office Furniture Company; the amount is an allowance for damaged but usable desks purchased on Invoice 4213, dated August 29.

 16 Purchased file cabinets for $2,656 plus a freight charge of $134 from Davis Corporation, Invoice 8066, dated September 11; the terms are 30 days net.

 20 Purchased electronic desk calculators for $1,100 from Apex Office Machines, Inc., Invoice 11011, dated September 15, net due and payable in 60 days.

 23 Purchased bond paper and copy machine paper for $8,500 plus a freight charge of $100 from Brown Paper Company, Invoice 6498, dated September 18; the terms are 1/10, n/30.

 28 Received Credit Memorandum 312 for $980 from Apex Office Machines, Inc., for defective calculators that were returned; the calculators were originally purchased on Invoice 11011, dated September 15.

 30 Purchased office chairs for $3,940 plus a freight charge of $170 from Zenn Furniture, Inc., Invoice 696, dated September 25, the terms are 2/10, n/30.

2. Print the September 3-30, 2016 journal.
3. Print the September 1-30, 2016 general ledger.
4. Print the Vendor Balance Detail report. (Substitute QuickBooks' Vendor Balance Detail report for the accounts payable subsidiary ledger and schedule of accounts payable.)
5. Back up. The suggested file name is **Problem 08.4A.QBM**.
6. **Analyze:** What total amount was recorded for purchases returns and allowances in the month of September? What percentage of total purchases does this represent? Use a blank piece of paper or the *Working Papers* to answer the analysis question.

Chapter 9 | Cash Receipts, Cash Payments, and Banking Procedures

In Chapter 9 of *College Accounting, 14e*, there are three QuickBooks problems.

➤ Problem 9.1A Entertainment Inc.: Journalizing cash receipts and posting to the general ledger.

➤ Problem 9.3A Awesome Sounds: Journalizing sales and cash receipts and posting to the general ledger.

➤ Problem 9.4A Bike and Hike Outlet: Journalizing purchases, cash payments, and purchases discounts; posting to the general ledger.

Chapter 9's QuickBooks activities demonstrate how to:

- Restore three QuickBooks problem templates.
- Journalize and post transactions.
- Print the journal.
- Print the general ledger.
- Print the income statement.
- Complete Problem 9.1A, Problem 9.3A, and Problem 9.4A.

GETTING STARTED: Problem 9.1A

Follow these steps to start QuickBooks and restore the Problem 09.1A.Entertainment Inc.QBM file.

1. Start QuickBooks.
2. If the menu bar shows a company name, click File; Open or Restore Company.
3. The Open or Restore Company window appears. Select Restore a portable file.
4. Click [Next]. The Open Portable Company File window appears. In the Look in field, go to the appropriate location for the Problem 09.1A.Entertainment Inc.QBM file. Click on the file to highlight it. Click [Open]. (*Hint:* You can also double-click on the file name.)
5. The Open or Restore Company window appears. Click [Next].

6. The Save Company File as window appears. Accept the default file name or change it slightly. Click 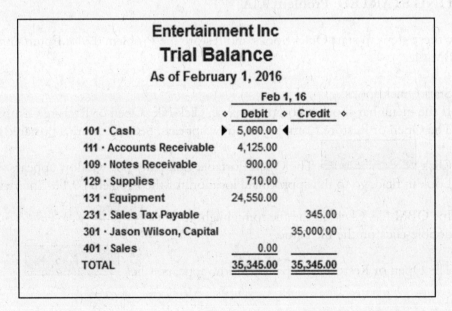 Save . When Entertainment Inc - QuickBooks Accountant 2014 appears, the file is restored.

7. Continue with the next section "My Company."

My Company

Before recording transactions for Entertainment Inc., look at the My Company information included on the Problem 09.1A.Entertainment Inc.QBM file.

1. From the Icon Bar, select ⟦My Company⟧. (*Or*, from the menu bar, select Company; My Company.) The My Company window appears.

2. To add your name to the Company Name field, click ⟦✎⟧. Close the My Company window.

Display the Trial Balance

Entertainment Inc. is a retail store that rents movies and sells music CDs over the Internet. The firm's cash receipts for February are listed on pages 57-59. The trial balance below shows each account balance in the general ledger.

Follow these steps to display Entertainment Inc. trial balance.

1. Go to the Report Center or Reports menu; Accountant & Taxes, Trial Balance.

2. Type **2/1/2016** in the From and To fields. Click ⟦Refresh⟧.

Entertainment Inc
Trial Balance
As of February 1, 2016

	Feb 1, 16	
	Debit	Credit
101 · Cash	5,060.00	
111 · Accounts Receivable	4,125.00	
109 · Notes Receivable	900.00	
129 · Supplies	710.00	
131 · Equipment	24,550.00	
231 · Sales Tax Payable		345.00
301 · Jason Wilson, Capital		35,000.00
401 · Sales	0.00	
TOTAL	35,345.00	35,345.00

3. In QuickBooks, an account balance is added for Equipment. This was done so that debit balances equal credit balances. Close the trial balance.

Journalizing and Posting Cash Receipts Transactions

Follow the steps below to journalize and post cash received from a customer.

Date   *Transaction*

Feb. 3   Received $600 from Danielle Pelzel, a credit customer, on account.

Instructions:

1. In the Customers area, click 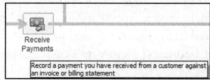. The Receive Payments window appears.
2. In the Received From field, select 114Danielle Pelzel for the customer, Danielle Pelzel.
3. Type **600** in the Amount field.
4. Type **2/3/2016** in the Date field.
5. In the Pmt. Method field, select Check.
6. In the Deposit to field, select Account No. 101, Cash.
7. Type **600** in the Payment field. Observe that the Amount Due shows 800.00. A checkmark is placed on that row. If not, click on it.
8. Observe that the Leave this as an underpayment field is selected. The Applied amount shows 600.00, the amount of this payment.

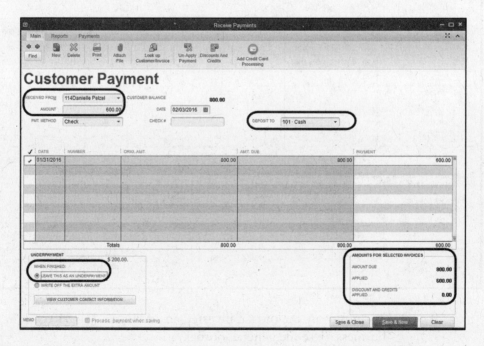

---

9. Click [Save & Close].

Required:

1. Journalize and post the February 5-28 transactions. When using QuickBooks Receive Payments feature, Account No. 101, Cash is automatically debited. If necessary, select the appropriate account(s) to credit. If there is *no* customer to select, type a description in the Name field.

Feb. 5   Received a cash refund of $130 for damaged supplies. (*Hint:* Select Company, Make General Journal Entries. Debit, Account No. 101 Cash; credit, Account No. 129 Supplies.)

7   Had cash sales of $5,800 plus sales tax of $464 during the first week of February; there was a cash shortage of $70. (*Hint:*. From the

Banking area of the Home page, select [Record Deposits]. To record this entry, refer to the Make Deposits window to record this entry.)

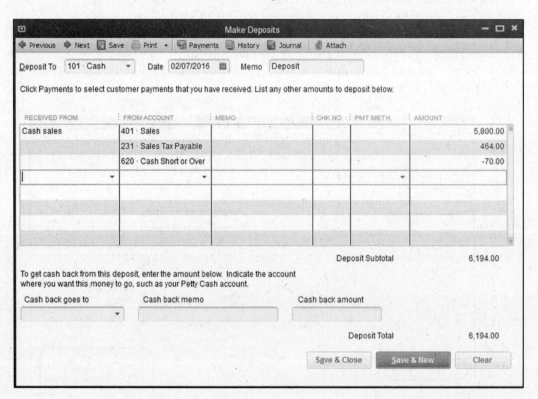

9   Jason Wilson, the owner, invested an additional $16,000 cash in the business. (Use the general journal.)

12	Received $480 from Kyela Jones, a credit customer, in payment of her account.
14	Had cash sales of $4,550 plus sales tax of $364 during the second week of February; there was an overage of $38. (*Hint:* Use Record Deposits.)
16	Received $550 from Sadie Nelson, a credit customer, to apply toward her account.
19	Received a check from Ketura Pittman to pay her $900 promissory note plus interest of $36. (Use Record Deposits. You do *not* have to complete the Received from fields.)
21	Had cash sales of $5,050 plus sales tax of $404 during the third week of February.
25	Alfred Herron, a credit customer, sent a check for $680 to pay the balance he owes.
28	Had cash sales of $5,100 plus sales tax of $408 during the fourth week of February; there was a cash shortage of $46.

2. Print the February 3-28, 2016 journal.
3. Print the February 1-28, 2016 general ledger.
4. Back up. The suggested file name is **Problem 09.1A.QBM**.
5. **Analyze**: What total accounts receivable were collected in February? (*Hint:* Look at the Customer Balance Detail report and add up the customer payments.) On a blank piece of paper or in the *Working Papers*, complete the analysis question.

GETTING STARTED: Problem 9.3A

Follow these steps to start QuickBooks and restore the Problem 09.3A.Awesome Sounds.QBM file.

Instructions:

1. Start QuickBooks.
2. If the menu bar shows a company name, click File; Open or Restore Company.
3. The Open or Restore Company window appears. Select Restore a portable file.
4. Click [Next]. The Open Portable Company File window appears. In the Look in field, go to the appropriate location for the Problem 09.3A.Awesome Sounds.QBM file. Click on the file to highlight it. Click [Open]. (*Hint:* You can also double-click on the file name.)
5. The Open or Restore Company window appears. Click [Next].
6. The Save Company File as window appears. Accept the default file name or change it slightly. Click [Save]. When Awesome Sounds - QuickBooks Accountant 2014 appears, the file is restored.
7. Continue with the next section "My Company."

My Company

Before recording transactions for Awesome Sounds, look at the My Company information included on the Problem 09.3A.Awesome Sounds.QBM file.

1. From the Icon Bar, select 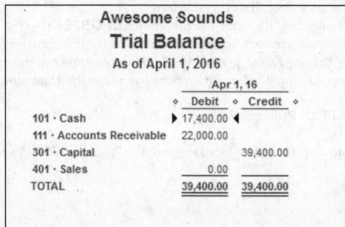 . (*Or,* from the menu bar, select Company; My Company.) The My Company window appears.

2. To add your name to the Company Name field, click ⬚. Close the My Company window.

Display the Trial Balance

The Trial Balance shown below lists the account balances in the general ledger accounts. Display the April 1, 2016 trial balance and compare it with the one shown below. These are the starting general ledger balances included on the Problem 09.3A.Awesome Sounds.QBM file.

Awesome Sounds
Trial Balance
As of April 1, 2016

	Apr 1, 16	
	Debit	Credit
101 · Cash	17,400.00	
111 · Accounts Receivable	22,000.00	
301 · Capital		39,400.00
401 · Sales	0.00	
TOTAL	39,400.00	39,400.00

Observe that QuickBooks' Capital balance is the result of the balances in Cash and Accounts Receivable.

Required:

Awesome Sounds is a wholesale business that sells musical instruments. Transactions involving sales and cash receipts for the firm during April 2016 are shown on pages 61-63.

1. Journalize and post the April 1 – 30 transactions. The April 3 transaction includes a receipt from a customer with terms of 2%, 10, Net 30 Days. This means that a sales discount is applied when the customer pays within 10 days. To complete that entry, remember to type the appropriate discount amount in the discount column.

April 1   Sold merchandise for $4,900 to Soprano Music Center; issued Invoice 9312 with terms of 2/10, n/30.

3   Received a check for $1,960 from Music Supply Store in payment of Invoice 6718 of March 25 ($2,000), less a cash discount ($40.00). (*Hint:* In the

Deposit To field, select 101, Cash. Select  to apply the cash discount. In the Discount field, select Account No. 452, Sales Discounts. Refer to the Discount and Credits window below and the Receive Payments window on the next page.

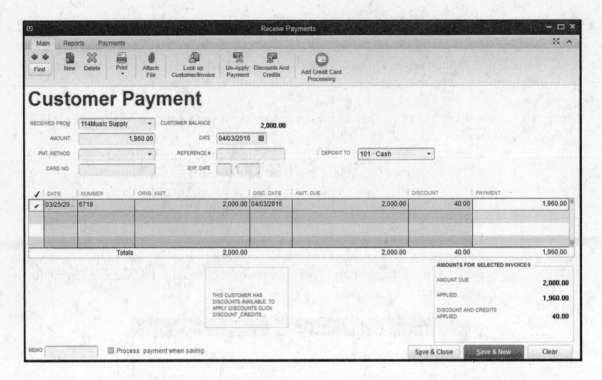

5   Sold merchandise for $1,825 in cash to a new customer who has not yet established credit. (*Hint:* Use Record Deposits; Received From, Cash sales.)

8   Sold merchandise for $5,500 to Music Warehouse, issued Invoice 9313 with terms of 2/10, n/30.

10   Soprano Music Center sent a check for $4,802 in payment of Invoice 9312 of April 1 ($4,900), less a cash discount ($98).

15   Accepted a return of damaged merchandise from Music Warehouse; issued Credit Memorandum 105 for $900; the original sale was made on Invoice 9313 of April 8. (*Hint:* Apply return to Invoice 9313.)

19   Sold merchandise for $11,500 to Eagleton Music Center; issued Invoice 9314 with terms of 2/10, n/30.

23   Collected $3,225 from Sounds From Yesterday for Invoice 6725 of March 25.

26   Accepted a two-month promissory note for $6,500 from Country Music Store in settlement of its overdue account; the note has an interest rate of 12 percent. (See the Make General Journal Entries window on the next page.)

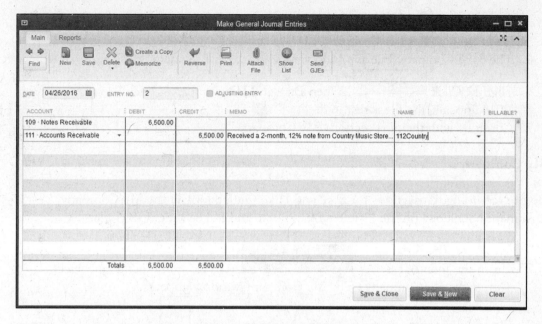

28   Received a check for $11,270 from Eagleton Music Center in payment of Invoice 9314, dated April 19 ($11,500), less a cash discount ($230).

30   Sold merchandise for $10,800 to Contemporary Sounds, Inc.; issued Invoice 9315 with terms of 2/10, n/30.

2. Print the April 1-30, 2016 journal.
3. Print the April 1-30, 2016 general ledger. (QB sales account includes sales returns.)
4. Back up. The suggested file name is **Problem 09.3A.QBM**.
5. **Analyze:** What total sales on account were made in the month of April, prior to any returns or allowances? On a blank piece of paper or in the *Working Papers*, complete the analysis question.

GETTING STARTED: Problem 9.4A

Follow these steps to start QuickBooks and restore the Problem 09.4A.Bike and Hike Outlet.QBM file.

Instructions:

1. Start QuickBooks.
2. If the menu bar shows a company name, click File; Open or Restore Company.
3. The Open or Restore Company window appears. Select Restore a portable file.

4. Click [Next]. The Open Portable Company File window appears. In the Look in field, go to the appropriate location for the Problem 09.4A.Bike and Hike Outlet.QBM file. Click on the file to highlight it. Click [Open]. (*Hint:* You can also double-click on the file name.)

5. The Open or Restore Company window appears. Click Next .

6. The Save Company File as window appears. Accept the default file name or change it slightly. Click Save . When Bike and Hike Outlet - QuickBooks Accountant 2014 appears, the file is restored.

7. Continue with the next section "My Company."

My Company

Before recording transactions for Bike and Hike Outlet, look at the My Company information included on the Problem 09.4A.Bike and Hike Outlet.QBM file.

1. From the Icon Bar, select My Company . (Or, from the menu bar, select Company; My Company.) The My Company window appears.

2. To add your name to the Company Name field, click . Close the My Company window.

Display the Trial Balance

Display the June 1, 2016 trial balance and compare it with the one shown below. These are the starting general ledger balances included on the Problem 09.4A.Bike and Hike Outlet.QBM file.

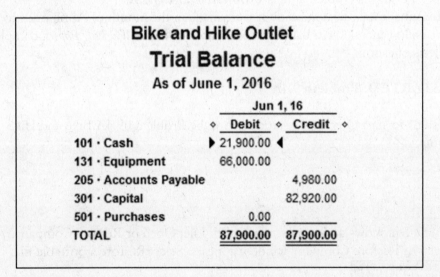

Bike and Hike Outlet
Trial Balance
As of June 1, 2016

	Jun 1, 16	
	Debit	Credit
101 · Cash	21,900.00	
131 · Equipment	66,000.00	
205 · Accounts Payable		4,980.00
301 · Capital		82,920.00
501 · Purchases	0.00	
TOTAL	87,900.00	87,900.00

Observe that QuickBooks' Capital balance is the result of the balances in Cash and Equipment, minus Accounts Payable.

Required:

The Bike and Hike Outlet is a retail store. Transactions involving purchases and cash payments for the firm during June 2016 are shown below and on pages 66-67.

1. Journalize and post the June 1 – 30, 2016 transactions.

June 1   Issued Check 1101 for $3,400 to pay the monthly rent. (*Hint:* Use the Write Checks feature. Uncheck Print Later, then type in the appropriate check number in the No. field. In the Pay to the Order of field, select Rent. In the Account field, select Account No. 611, Rent Expense).

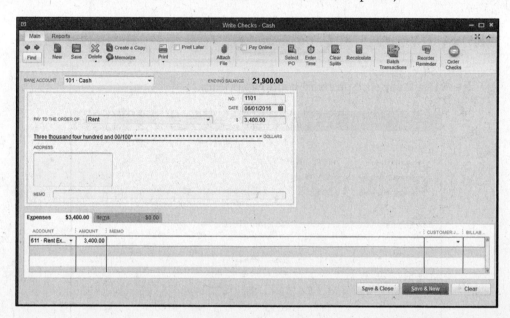

3   Purchased merchandise for $3,100 from Perfect Fit Shoe Shop, Invoice 746, dated June 1; the terms are 2/10, n/30.

5   Purchased new store equipment for $5,500 from Middleton Company, Invoice 9067 dated June 4, net payable in 30 days. (*Hint:* Make sure Account No. 131, Equipment is debited.)

7   Issued Check 1102 for $1,570 to Leisure Wear Clothing Company, a creditor, in payment of Invoice 3342 of May 9. (*Hint:* To complete this transaction, use the Vendors; Pay Bills feature. If necessary, select Show all bills; put a checkmark next to the 513Lieisure bill; and type **6/7/2016** in the Payment Date field.) Select Assign check number. Click **Pay Selected Bills**. Type **1102** in the Check No. field.

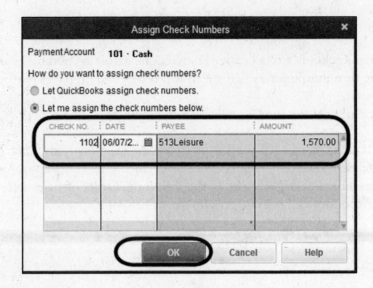

The Payment Summary window appears.

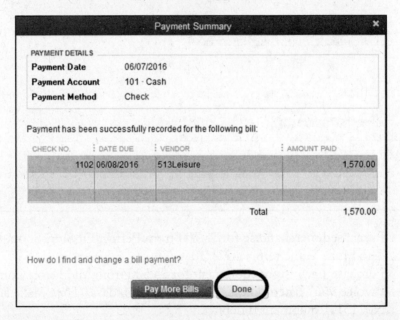

8   Issued Check 1103 for $3,038 to Perfect Fit Shoe Shop, a creditor, in payment of Invoice 746 dated June 1 ($3,100), less a cash discount ($62). On the Pay Bills window, click on the radio button next to Assign check number.

Click [Set Discount]. In the Discount Account field, select Account No. 504, Purchase Discounts.

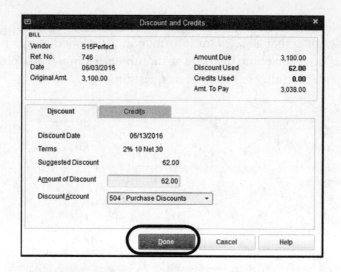

Click **Pay Selected Bills** . Type **1103** in the Check No. field. Observe the
Amount is 3,038.00. Click OK. The Payment Summary window appears.
Click Done.

12   Purchased merchandise for $2,300 from Juanda's Coat Shop, Invoice 9922,
      dated June 9, net due and payable in 30 days.
15   Issued Check 1104 for $238 to pay the monthly telephone bill. (*Hint:* If
      necessary, type the appropriate check number, 1104, in the No. field.)
18   Received Credit Memorandum 203 for $800 from Juanda's Coat Shop for
      defective goods that were returned; the original purchase was made on
      Invoice 9922 dated June 9.
21   Purchased new store equipment for $10,500 from Warren Company; issued a
      three-month promissory note with interest at 12 percent. (Use the General
      Journal; debit Account No. 131 Equipment; credit Account No. 201 Notes
      Payable.)
23   Purchased merchandise for $6,400 from The Motor Speedway, Invoice 1927,
      dated June 20; terms of 2/10, n/30.
25   Issued Check 1105 for $1,500 to Juanda's Coat Shop, a creditor, in payment
      of Invoice 7416 dated May 28.
28   Issued Check 1106 for $6,272 to The Motor Speedway, a creditor, in
      payment of Invoice 1927 of June 20 ($6,400), less a cash discount ($128).
30   Purchased merchandise for $2,080 from Jogging Shoes Store, Invoice 4713,
      dated June 26; the terms are 1/10, n/30.
30   Issued Check 1107 for $5,800 to pay the monthly salaries of the employees.
      (*Hint:* If necessary, type the appropriate check number.)

2. Print the June 1-30, 2016 journal.
3. Print the June 1-30, 2016 general ledger.

4. Back up. The suggested file name is **Problem 09.4A.QBM**.
5. **Analyze**: Assuming that all relevant information is included in this problem, what total liabilities does the company have at month-end? On a blank piece of paper or in the *Working Papers*, complete the analysis question

Chapter 11

Payroll Taxes, Deposits, and Reports

In Chapter 11 of *College Accounting, 14e*, there is one QuickBooks problem.

➤ Problem 11.2A Mark Consulting Company: Computing employer's social security tax, Medicare tax, and unemployment taxes.

Chapter 11's QuickBooks activities demonstrate how to:

- Restore one QuickBooks problem template.
- Journalize and post payroll transactions.
- Print the journal.
- Complete Problem 11.2A.

GETTING STARTED: Problem 11.2A

Follow these steps to start QuickBooks and restore the Problem 11.2A.Mark Consulting Company.QBM file.

Instructions:

1. Start QuickBooks.
2. If the menu bar shows a company name, click File; Open or Restore Company.
3. The Open or Restore Company window appears. Select Restore a portable file.
4. Click [Next]. The Open Portable Company File window appears. In the Look in field, go to the appropriate location for the Problem 11.2A.Mark Consulting Company.QBM file. Click on the file to highlight it. Click [Open]. (*Hint:* You can also double-click on the file name.)
5. The Open or Restore Company window appears. Click [Next].
6. The Save Company File as window appears. Accept the default file name or change it slightly. Click [Save]. When Mark Consulting Company - QuickBooks Accountant 2014 appears, the file is restored.
7. Continue with the next section "My Company."

My Company

Before recording transactions for Mark Consulting Company, look at the My Company information included on the Problem 11.2A.Mark Consulting Company.QBM file.

1. From the Icon Bar, select [My Company]. (*Or,* from the menu bar, select Company; My Company.) The My Company window appears.

2. To add your name to the Company Name field, click [pencil icon]. Close the My Company window.

Journalizing and Posting Payroll Taxes

A payroll summary for Mark Consulting Company, owned by Mark Fonke, for the quarter ending June 30, 2016, appears below. The firm made the required tax deposits as follows:

- For April taxes, paid on May 15.
- For May taxes, paid on June 17.

Date Wages Paid		Total Earnings	Social Security Tax Deducted	Medicare Tax Deducted	Income Tax Withheld
April	8	$ 3,400.00	$ 210.80	$ 49.30	$ 338.00
	15	3,700.00	229.40	53.65	365.00
	22	4,100.00	254.20	59.45	338.00
	29	4,400.00	272.80	63.80	436.00
		$15,600.00	$ 967.20	$226.20	$1,477.00
May	5	$ 3,200.00	$ 198.40	$ 46.40	318.00
	12	3,400.00	210.80	49.30	338.00
	19	3,400.00	210.80	49.30	338.00
	26	4,400.00	272.80	63.80	436.00
		$14,400.00	$ 892.80	$208.80	$1,430.00
June	2	$ 3,700.00	$ 229.40	$ 53.65	$ 365.00
	9	3,400.00	210.80	49.30	338.00
	16	4,400.00	272.80	63.80	436.00
	23	3,400.00	210.80	49.30	338.00
	30	3,200.00	198.40	46.40	318.00
		$18,100.00	$1,122.20	$262.45	$1,795.00
Total		$48,100.00	$2,982.20	$697.45	$4,702.00

1. Using the tax rates given below, and assuming that all earnings are taxable, make the general journal entry on April 8, 2016, to record the employer's payroll tax expense on the payroll ending that date.

   Social Security   6.2 percent
   Medicare   1.45
   FUTA   0.6
   SUTA   5.4

2. Journalize and post the entries in the general journal to record deposit of the employee income tax withheld and the social security and Medicare taxes (employee and employer shares) on May 15 for April taxes and on June 17 for May taxes.

Required:

1. Print the April 8-June 17, 2016 journal.
2. Back up. The suggested file name is **Problem 11.2A.QBM**.
3. **Analyze:** How were the amounts for Income Tax Withheld determined? Use a blank piece of paper or the *Working Papers* to answer the analysis question.

Chapter 12

Accruals, Deferrals, and the Worksheet

In Chapter 12 of *College Accounting, 14e*, there is one QuickBooks problem.

➤ Problem 12.2A Sean McConnell: Recording adjustments for accrued and prepaid expense items and unearned income.

Chapter 12's QuickBooks activities demonstrate how to:

- Restore one QuickBooks problem template.
- Journalize and post transactions.
- Print the journal.
- Complete Problem 12.2A.

GETTING STARTED: Problem 12.2A

Follow these steps to start QuickBooks and restore the Problem 12.2A.Sean McConnell.QBM file.

Instructions:

1. Start QuickBooks.
2. If the menu bar shows a company name, click File; Open or Restore Company.
3. The Open or Restore Company window appears. Select Restore a portable file.
4. Click [Next]. The Open Portable Company File window appears. In the Look in field, go to the appropriate location for the Problem 12.2A.Sean

   McConnell.QBM file. Click on the file to highlight it. Click [Open]. (*Hint:* You can also double-click on the file name.)

5. The Open or Restore Company window appears. Click [Next].
6. The Save Company File as window appears. Accept the default file name or change it

   slightly. Click [Save]. When Sean McConnell - QuickBooks Accountant 2014 appears, the file is restored.
7. Continue with the next section "My Company."

My Company

Before recording transactions for Sean McConnell, look at the My Company information included on the Problem 12.2A.Sean McConnell.QBM file.

1. From the Icon Bar, select **My Company**. (*Or,* from the menu bar, select Company; My Company.) The My Company window appears.

2. To add your name to the Company Name field, click [icon]. Close the My Company window.

Required:

On July 1, 2016, Sean McConnell established his own accounting practice. Selected transactions for the first few days of July follow.

July	1	Signed a lease for an office and issued Check 101 for $14,700 to pay the rent in advance for six months.
	1	Borrowed money from First National Bank by issuing a four-month, 9 percent note for $40,000; received $38,800 because the bank deducted the interest in advance.
	1	Signed an agreement with Young Corp. to provide accounting and tax services for one year at $7,000 per month; received the entire fee of $84,000 in advance.
	1	Purchased office equipment for $15,900 from Office Outfitters; issued a two-month, 12 percent note in payment. The equipment is estimated to have a useful life of five years and a $1,500 salvage value. The equipment will be depreciated using the straight-line method.
	1	Purchased a one-year insurance policy and issued Check 102 for $1,740 to pay the entire premium.
	3	Purchased office furniture for $16,080 from Office Warehouse; issued Check 103 for $8,480 and agreed to pay the balance in 60 days. The equipment has an estimated useful life of four years and a $1,200 salvage value. The office furniture will be depreciated using the straight-line method.
	5	Purchased office supplies for $2,010 with Check 104. Assume $900 of supplies are on hand July 31, 2016.

1. Journalize and post the July 1-5, 2016 transactions in the general journal. Omit descriptions. Assume that the firm initially records prepaid expenses as assets and unearned income as a liability.
2. Journalize and post the adjusting journal entries that must be made on July 31, 2016. (*Hint:* On the General Journal Entry window, select Adjusting entry.)
3. Print the July 1-31, 2016 journal.

4. Back up. The suggested file name is **Problem 12.2A.QBM**.
5. **Analyze:** What balance should be reflected in Unearned Accounting Fees at July 31, 2016? Use a blank piece of paper or the *Working Papers* to answer the analysis question.

<table>
<tr><td>

Chapter
13

</td><td>

Financial Statements and Closing Procedures

</td></tr>
</table>

In Chapter 13 of *College Accounting, 14e*, there are three QuickBooks problems.

➤ Problem 13.1A Quality Hardwoods Company: Preparing classified financial statements.

➤ Problem 13.5A Victoria Company: Journalizing adjusting and reversing entries.

➤ Mini-Practice Set 2 The Fashion Rack: Merchandising Business Accounting Cycle.

Chapter 13's QuickBooks activities demonstrate how to:

- Restore three QuickBooks problem templates.
- Journalize and post adjusting entries
- Journalize and post reversing entries
- Print the journal.
- Print the income statement and balance sheet.
- Complete Problem 13.1A, Problem 13.5A, and Mini-Practice Set 2.

GETTING STARTED: Problem 13.1A

Follow these steps to start QuickBooks and restore the Problem 13.1A.Quality Hardwoods Company.QBM file.

Instructions:

1. Start QuickBooks.
2. If the menu bar shows a company name, click File; Open or Restore Company.
3. The Open or Restore Company window appears. Select Restore a portable file.

4. Click **Next**. The Open Portable Company File window appears. In the Look in field, go to the appropriate location for the Problem 13.1A.Quality

   Hardwoods Company.QBM file. Click on the file to highlight it. Click **Open**. (*Hint:* You can also double-click on the file name.)

5. The Open or Restore Company window appears. Click  **Next**.

6. The Save Company File as window appears. Accept the default file name or change it slightly. Click Save. When Quality Hardwoods Company - QuickBooks Accountant 2014 appears, the file is restored.

7. Continue with the next section "My Company."

My Company

Before recording transactions for the Quality Hardwoods Company, look at the My Company information included on the Problem 13.1A.Quality Hardwoods Company.QBM file.

1. From the Icon Bar, select My Company. (*Or,* from the menu bar, select Company; My Company.) The My Company window appears.

2. To add your name to the Company Name field, click ✏️. Close the My Company window.

Printing the Financial Statements

Substitute QB P&L standard report for the income statement. Observe how QB organizes the P&L into the following sections: Ordinary Income/Expense, which includes Income, Cost of Goods Sold, and Expenses. There is also an Other Income/Expense section.

A difference between the textbook's classified income statement and QB P&L is the way the textbook computes Cost of Goods Sold. QuickBooks' P&L does *not* include beginning and ending inventory. QuickBooks' P&L reports revenues and expenses only—Merchandise Inventory is an asset and is reported on the Balance Sheet. For that reason, QuickBooks' P&L reports $145,640 as the Net Income, which is $10,000 more than the textbook. On textbook page 467, there is a debit and credit amount shown in the Income Summary account. The difference is $10,000, which is also the difference in the Net Income reported by QuickBooks.

Income Summary, Account No. 399		
234,000		224,000
	Difference	10,000
234,000		234,000

$145,640 (QuickBooks' net income)
− 10,000
$135,640 (Net income for the Year)

Required:

Quality Hardwoods Company distributes hardwood products to small furniture manufacturers. The adjusted trial balance data is shown on the December 31, 2016 trial balance. You may want to look at the December 1-31, 2016 trial balance included on the Problem 13.1A.Quality Hardwoods Company.QBM file.

1. Go the Report Center or the Reports menu; select Company & Financial, Profit & Loss Standard for 12/1/2016 to 12/31/2016.
2. Make the selections to print the Profit & Loss report. (The Net Income amount reported on QB P&L agrees with the net income reported on the balance sheet.)
3. Select Reports; Company & Financial, Balance Sheet Standard for 12/31/2016.
4. Make the selections to print the balance sheet. The Equity section of QuickBooks' balance sheet can be used for the Statement of Owner's Equity.
5. Back up. The suggested file name is **Problem 13.1A.QBM**.
6. **Analyze:** What is the current ratio for this business? Use a blank piece of paper or the *Working Papers* to complete the analysis question.

GETTING STARTED: Problem 13.5A

Follow these steps to start QuickBooks and restore the Problem 13.5A.Victoria Company.QBM file.

Instructions:

1. Start QuickBooks.
2. If the menu bar shows a company name, click File; Open or Restore Company.
3. The Open or Restore Company window appears. Select Restore a portable file.
4. Click [Next]. The Open Portable Company File window appears. In the Look in field, go to the appropriate location for the Problem 13.5.Victoria Company.QBM file. Click on the file to highlight it. Click [Open]. (*Hint:* You can also double-click on the file name.)
5. The Open or Restore Company window appears. Click [Next].
6. The Save Company File as window appears. Accept the default file name or change it slightly. Click [Save]. When Victoria Company - QuickBooks Accountant 2014 appears, the file is restored.
7. Continue with the next section "My Company."

My Company

Before recording transactions for Victoria Company, look at the My Company information included on the Problem 13.5A.Victoria Company.QBM file.

1. From the Icon Bar, select [My Company]. (*Or,* from the menu bar, select Company; My Company.) The My Company window appears.

2. To add your name to the Company Name field, click [pencil icon]. Close the My Company window.

Required:

The data below concerns adjustments to be made at Victoria Company.

1. Journalize and post the December 31, 2016 adjusting entries.

   a. On October 1, 2016, the firm signed a lease for a warehouse and paid rent of $20,700 in advance for a six-month period.
   b. On December 31, 2016, an inventory of supplies showed that items costing $1,940 were on hand. The balance of the Supplies account was $11,620.
   c. A depreciation schedule for the firm's equipment shows that a total of $9,200 should be charged off as depreciation for 2016.
   d. On December 31, 2016, the firm owed salaries of $5,400 that will not be paid until January 2017.
   e. On December 31, 2016, the firm owed the employer's social security (6.2 percent) and Medicare (1.45 percent) taxes on all accrued salaries.
   f. On September 1, 2016, the firm received a five-month, 6 percent note for $5,500 from a customer with an overdue balance.

2. Back up. The suggested file name is **Problem 13.5A.Adjusted.QBM**.
3. Journalize and post the January 1, 2017 reversing entries.
4. Print the December 31, 2016 through January 1, 2017 journal.
5. Back up. The suggested file name is **Problem 13.5A.Reversed.QBM**.
6. **Analyze:** After the adjusting entries have been posted, what is the balance of the Prepaid Rent account on January 1, 2017? Use a blank piece of paper or the *Working Papers* to complete the analysis question.

MINI-PRACTICE SET 2: MERCHANDISING BUSINESS ACCOUNTING CYCLE

Follow these steps to start QuickBooks and restore the Mini Practice Set 2.The Fashion Rack.QBM file.

Instructions:

1. Start QuickBooks.
2. If the menu bar shows a company name, click File; Open or Restore Company.
3. The Open or Restore Company window appears. Select Restore a portable file.

4. Click **Next**. The Open Portable Company File window appears. In the Look in field, go to the appropriate location for the Mini Practice Set 2.The Fashion Rack.QBM file. Click on the file to highlight it. Click **Open**. (*Hint:* You can also double-click on the file name.)

5. The Open or Restore Company window appears. Click **Next**.

6. The Save Company File as window appears. Accept the default file name or change it slightly. Click **Save**. When The Fashion Rack - QuickBooks Accountant 2014 appears, the file is restored.

7. Continue with the next section "My Company."

My Company

Before recording transactions for The Fashion Rack, look at the My Company information included on the Mini Practice Set 2.The Fashion Rack.QBM file.

1. From the Icon Bar, select **My Company**. (*Or,* from the menu bar, select Company; My Company.) The My Company window appears.

2. To add your name to the Company Name field, click [pencil icon]. Close the My Company window.

The Fashion Rack is a retail merchandising business that sells brand-name clothing at discount prices. The firm is owned and managed by Teresa Lojay who started the business on April 1, 2016. This project will give you an opportunity to put your knowledge of accounting into practice as you handle the accounting work of The Fashion Rack during the month of October 2016.

The Fashion Rack has a monthly accounting period. Display or print QuickBooks' chart of accounts and compare it to the one shown on the next page.

The Fashion Rack Chart of Accounts

Assets
101 Cash
111 Accounts Receivable
112 Allowance for Doubtful Accounts
121 Merchandise Inventory
131 Supplies
133 Prepaid Insurance
135 Prepaid Advertising
141 Equipment
142 Accumulated Depreciation—Equipment

Liabilities
203 Accounts Payable
221 Social Security Tax Payable
222 Medicare Tax Payable
223 Employee Income Tax Payable
225 Federal Unemployment Tax Payable
227 State Unemployment Tax Payable
229 Salaries Payable
231 Sales Tax Payable

Owner's Equity
301 Teresa Lojay, Capital
302 Teresa Lojay, Drawing
399 Income Summary

Revenues
401 Sales
402 Sales Returns and Allowances

Cost of Goods Sold
501 Purchases
502 Freight In
503 Purchases Returns and Allowances
504 Purchases Discounts

Expenses
611 Advertising Expense
614 Depreciation Expense—Equipment
617 Insurance Expense
620 Uncollectible Accounts Expense
623 Janitorial Services Expense
626 Payroll Taxes Expense
629 Rent Expense
632 Salaries Expense
635 Supplies Expense
638 Telephone Expense
644 Utilities Expense

The September 30, 2016 postclosing trial balance is shown on the next page. These amounts represent the beginning balances as of October 1, 2016. Display or print the October 1, 2016 trial balance and compare with it with the postclosing trial balance on page 83.

The Fashion Rack		
Postclosing Trial Balance		
September 30, 2016		
Account Name	**Debit**	**Credit**
Cash	59,800.00	
Accounts Receivable	6,210.00	
Allowance for Doubtful Accounts		420.00
Merchandise Inventory	88,996.00	
Supplies	4,100.00	
Prepaid Insurance	8,400.00	
Equipment	83,000.00	
Accumulated Depreciation-Equipment		7,050.00
Accounts Payable		18,300.00
Social Security Tax Payable		702.00
Medicare Tax Payable		162.00
Employee Income Tax Payable		1,020.00
Federal Unemployment Tax Payable		512.00
State Unemployment Tax Payable		1,268.00
Sales Tax Payable		17,820.00
Teresa Lojay, Capital		203,252.00
Totals	250,506.00	250,506.00

The account balances for vendors are shown below. Display or print the Vendor Balance Detail report and compare to the schedule of accounts payable shown below.

The Fashion Rack	
Schedule of Accounts Payable	
September 30, 2016	
A Fashion Statement	7,830.00
Classy Threads	1,700.00
Today's Woman	8,770.00
Total	18,300.00

The account balances for customers are shown below. Display or print the Customer Balance Detail report and compare to the schedule of accounts receivable shown below.

The Fashion Rack	
Schedule of Accounts Receivable	
September 30, 2016	
Jennifer Brown	795.00
Megan Greening	520.00
James Helmer	832.00
Emma Maldonado	232.00
Jim Price	1,621.00
Dimitri Sayegh	510.00
Emily Tran	1,700.00
Total	6,210.00

DATE	TRANSACTIONS

Oct 1   Issued Check 601 for $4,200 to pay City Properties the monthly rent.
(*Hint*: Use Write Checks. Uncheck the Print Later box then type **601** in the
No. field. Type **City Properties** in the Pay to the Order of field; press <Tab>.
When the Name Not found window appears, click Quick Add. On the Select
Name Type field, select Other; click OK.)

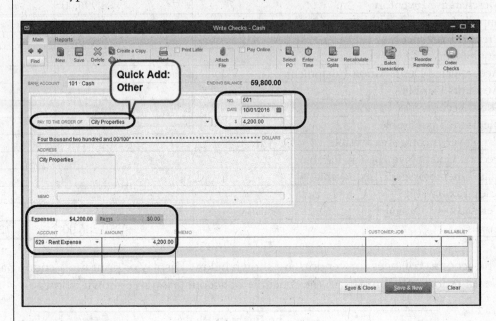

1   Signed a three-month radio advertising contract with Cable Station KOTU for
$4,800; issued Check 602 to pay the full amount in advance.

2   Received $520 from Megan Greening, a credit customer, in payment of her
account.

2   Issued Check 603 for $17,820 to remit the sales tax owed for July through
September to the State Tax Commission.

2   Issued Check 604 for $7,673.40 to A Fashion Statement, a creditor, in
payment of Invoice 9387 ($7,830), less a cash discount ($156.60). (*Hint:* On
the Pay Bills window, select Assign check number *and* select Set Discount.
Type **156.60** in the Amount of discount field. In the Discount Account field,
select Account No. 504 Purchases Discounts.

The Pay Bills window is shown on the next page.

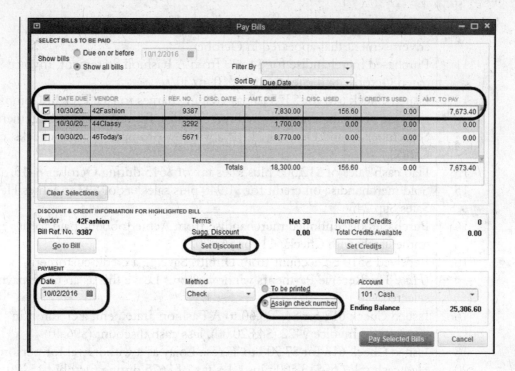

After selecting Pay Selected Bills, the Assign Check Numbers window appears. Type **604** in the Check No. field; click OK; then click Done.)

3   Sold merchandise on credit for $2,480 plus sales tax of $124 to Dimitri Sayegh, Sales Slip 241. (*Hint:* Type the Sales Slip Number in the Invoice # field. Remember to record sales tax.)

4   Issued Check 605 for $1,050 to BMX Supply Co. for supplies.

4   Issued Check 606 for $8,594.60 to Today's Woman, a creditor, in payment of Invoice 5671 ($8,770), less a cash discount ($175.40).

5   Collected $1,700.00 on account from Emily Tran, a credit customer.

5   Accepted a return of merchandise from Dimitri Sayegh. The merchandise was originally sold on Sales Slip 241, dated October 3; issued Credit Memorandum 18 for $630, which includes sales tax of $30. (*Hint:* Use Refunds & Credits. QuickBooks debits Account No. 401, Sales for sales returns. Remember to Apply to an Invoice No. 241.)

5   Issued Check 607 for $1,666 to Classy Threads, a creditor, in payment of Invoice 3292 ($1,700), less a cash discount ($34).

6   Had cash sales of $18,600 plus sales tax of $930 during October 1–6. (*Hint:* Use Record Deposits.)

8   Received a check from James Helmer, a credit customer, for $832 to pay the balance he owes.

8   Issued Check 608 for $1,884 to deposit social security tax ($702), Medicare tax ($162), and federal income tax withholding ($1,020) from the September payroll.

9   Sold merchandise on credit for $2,050 plus sales tax of $102.50 to Emma Maldonado, Sales Slip 242.

Oct	10	Issued Check 609 for $1,445 to pay *The City Daily* for a newspaper advertisement that appeared in October.
	11	Purchased merchandise for $4,820 from A Fashion Statement, Invoice 9422, dated October 8; the terms are 2/10, n/30.
	12	Issued Check 610 for $375 to pay freight charges to Ace Freight Company, the trucking company that delivered merchandise from A Fashion Statement on September 27 and October 11. (If a window prompts to order checks, click Cancel.)
	13	Had cash sales of $12,300 plus sales tax of $615 during October 8–13.
	15	Sold merchandise on credit for $1,940 plus sales tax of $97 to James Helmer, Sales Slip 243.
	16	Purchased discontinued merchandise from Acme Jobbers; paid for it immediately with Check 611 for $6,420.
	16	Received $510 on account from Dimitri Sayegh, a credit customer. (*Hint:* The Receive Payments window shows Leave this as an underpayment selected.)
	16	Issued Check 612 for $4,723.60 to A Fashion Statement, a creditor, in payment of Invoice 9422 ($4,820.00), less cash discount ($96.40).
	18	Issued Check 613 for $7,200 to Teresa Lojay as a withdrawal for personal use.
	20	Had cash sales of $13,500 plus sales tax of $675 during October 15–20.
	22	Issued Check 614 to City Utilities for $1,112 to pay the monthly electric bill.
	24	Sold merchandise on credit for $820 plus sales tax of $41 to Megan Greening, Sales Slip 244.
	25	Purchased merchandise for $3,380 from Classy Threads, Invoice 3418, dated October 23; the terms are 2/10, n/30.
	26	Issued Check 615 to Regional Telephone for $780 to pay the monthly telephone bill.
	27	Had cash sales of $14,240 plus sales tax of $712 during October 22–27.
	29	Received Credit Memorandum 175 for $430 from Classy Threads Inc. for defective goods that were returned. The original purchase was made on Invoice 3418, dated October 25. (*Hint:* Select Pay bill, Credit. Remember to select Account No. 503, Purchases Returns & Allowances.)
	29	Sold merchandise on credit for $3,120 plus sales tax of $156 to Emily Tran, Sales Slip 245.
	29	Recorded the October payroll. The records prepared by the payroll service show the following totals: earnings, $10,800; social security, $702.00; Medicare, $162.00; income tax, $1,020; and net pay, $8,916. The excess withholdings corrected an error made in withholdings in September. (*Hint:* Record this transaction in the General Journal.)
	29	Recorded the employer's payroll taxes, which were calculated by the payroll service: social security, $702; Medicare, $162; federal unemployment tax, $118; and state unemployment tax, $584. This, too, reflects an understatement of taxes recorded in September and corrected in this month. (*Hint:* Record this transaction in the General Journal.)
	30	Purchased merchandise for $4,020 from Today's Woman, Invoice 5821, dated October 26; the terms are 1/10, n/30.

31	Issued Checks 616 through 619, totaling $8,916.00, to employees to pay October payroll. For the sake of simplicity, enter the total of the checks on single line. (*Hint:* Type **616-619** for the check number.)
31	Issued Check 620 for $475 to Handy Janitors for October janitorial services. (*Hint:* Type **620** for the check number.)
31	Had cash sales of $1,700 plus sales tax of $85 for October 29–31.

Required:

1. Journalize and post October 1-31, 2016 transactions. Refer to pages 84-87.
2. Print the Customer Balance Detail and Vendor Balance Detail reports.
3. Backup. The suggested file name is **Mini Practice Set 2.October.QBM**. (*Hint:* If you print an unadjusted trial balance, the balance in Account No. 401, Sales, is $70,150, which reflects the sales return made on October 5 of $600. QuickBooks debits Account No. 401, Sales, for customer returns. QB does *not* use Sales Returns and Allowances.)
4. Journalize and post the following adjustments as of October 31, 2016. (*Hint:* On the Make General Journal Entries window, click on the box next to Adjusting Entry.)

   a. During October, the firm had net credit sales of $9,810. From experience with similar businesses, the previous accountant had estimated that 1.0 percent of the firm's net credit sales would result in uncollectible accounts. Record an adjustment for the expected loss from uncollectible accounts for the month of October.
   b. On October 31, an inventory of the supplies showed that items costing $3,240 were on hand. Record an adjustment for the supplies used in October.
   c. On September 30, 2016, the firm purchased a six-month insurance policy for $8,400. Record an adjustment for the expired insurance for October.
   d. On October 1, the firm signed a three-month advertising contract for $4,800 with a local cable television station and paid the full amount in advance. Record an adjustment for the expired advertising for October.
   e. On April 1, 2016, the firm purchased equipment for $83,000. The equipment was estimated to have a useful life of five years and a salvage value of $12,500. Record an adjustment for depreciation on the equipment for October.
   f. Based on a physical count, ending merchandise inventory was determined to be $81,260. Record the following adjusting entry in the general journal. The author suggests the adjusting entry shown below to accommodate for the difference between beginning and ending inventory: $88,996 - 81,260 = $7,736.

Account No.	Description	Debit	Credit
399	Income Summary	7,736.00	
121	Merchandise Inventory		7,736.00

Note: Check with your instructor for his or her preference. There are various ways to show the difference between manual and computerized accounting.

5. Print the adjusted trial balance.

6. Print the Profit & Loss (Standard), balance sheet (Standard). On QuickBooks' Profit & Loss, beginning and ending merchandise inventory is not shown. Merchandise inventory is an asset and is reported on the balance sheet. On QuickBooks' Profit & Loss, Net Income is $25,466.30. This difference occurs because Merchandise Inventory is not shown on QuickBooks' profit and loss statement. The textbook or *Working Papers* reports $17,730.30 as the net income.

QuickBooks' net income	25,466.30
Textbook/*Working Papers* net income	17,730.30
Difference	$7,736.00

October 1 Merchandise Inventory	88,996.00
October 31 Merchandise Inventory	81,260.00
Difference	$7,736.00

7. Backup. The suggested file name is **Mini Practice Set 2.Adjusted**.
8. Journalize and post the closing entries. Refer to QuickBooks' Adjusted Trial Balance and Profit & Loss to complete the closing entries. (*Hint:* The balance in Account No. 401, Sales, is $70,150. Remember to close the Net Income of $25,466.30 reported on QuickBooks' Profit & Loss. Close the balance in Account No. 399, Income Summary, to Account No. 301, Teresa Lojay Capital.)

Account No.	Description	Debit	Credit
301	Teresa Lojay, Capital	7,736.00	
399	Income Summary		7,736.00

9. Print the October 1-31, 2016 journal.
10. Print the October 1-31, 2016 general ledger.
11. Print the postclosing trial balance.
12. Backup. The suggested file name is **Mini Practice Set 2.Closed**.

Chapter 15

Accounts Receivable and Uncollectible Accounts

In Chapter 15 of *College Accounting, 14e*, there are three QuickBooks problems.

➢ Problem 15.1A Montana Leather Products: Estimating and recording uncollectible accounts transactions on the basis of sales.

➢ Problem 15.2.A Lucero Company: Estimating and recording uncollectible account transactions on the basis of accounts receivable.

➢ Problem 15.4A Pullman Company: Recording uncollectible account transactions under the direct charge-off method.

Chapter 15's QuickBooks activities demonstrate how to:

- Restore three QuickBooks problem templates.
- Journalize and post transactions.
- Print the journal.
- Complete Problem 15.1A, Problem 15.2A, and Problem 15.4A.

GETTING STARTED: Problem 15.1A

Follow these steps to start QuickBooks and restore the Problem 15.1A.Montana Leather Products.QBM file.

Instructions:

1. Start QuickBooks.
2. If the menu bar shows a company name, click File; Open or Restore Company.
3. The Open or Restore Company window appears. Select Restore a portable file.
4. Click **Next**. The Open Portable Company File window appears. In the Look in field, go to the appropriate location for the Problem 15.1A.Montana Leather Products.QBM file. Click on the file to highlight it. Click . (*Hint:* You can also double-click on the file name.)
5. The Open or Restore Company window appears. Click **Next**.

6. The Save Company File as window appears. Accept the default file name or change it slightly. Click [Save] . When Montana Leather Products - QuickBooks Accountant 2014 appears, the file is restored.
7. Continue with the next section "My Company."

My Company

Before recording transactions for the Montana Leather Products, look at the My Company information included on the Problem 15.1A.Montana Leather Products.QBM file.

1. From the Icon Bar, select [My Company] . (*Or,* from the menu bar, select Company; My Company.) The My Company window appears.

2. To add your name to the Company Name field, click [✎] . Close the My Company window.

Montana Leather Products sells leather clothing at both wholesale and retail. The company has found there is a higher rate of uncollectible accounts from retail credit sales than from wholesale credit sales. Montana computes its estimated loss from uncollectible accounts at the end of each year. The amount is based on the rates of loss that the firm has developed from experience for each division. A separate computation is made for each of the two types of sales. The firm uses the percentage of net credit sales method.

As of December 31, 2016, Accounts Receivable has a balance of $402,000, and Allowance for Doubtful Accounts has a debit balance of $426. These amounts are shown on the 15.1A.Montana Leather Products.QBM file's trial balance. You may want to display the December 31, 2016 trial balance to see these amounts.

The following table provides a breakdown of the credit sales for the year 2016 and the estimated rates of loss.

Category	Amount	Estimated Rate of Loss
Wholesale	$2,140,000	0.6%
Retail	599,000	1.1%

Required:

1. Restore the Problem 15.1A.Montana Leather Products.QBM file.
2. Compute the estimated amount of uncollectible accounts expense for each of the two categories of net credit sales for the year.

3. Journalize and post an adjusting entry in the general journal to provide for the estimated uncollectible accounts on December 31, 2016. Use Uncollectible Accounts Expense.

4. Show how Accounts Receivable and Allowance for Doubtful Accounts should appear on the balance sheet of Montana Leather Products as of December 31, 2016. (*Hint:* Display or print QB balance sheet; *or*, complete this instruction using a blank piece of paper or the *Working Papers*. QuickBooks' balance sheet shows an account balance for Accounts Receivable/Delphi Clothiers.)

5. Back up. The suggested file name is **Problem 15.1A.Adjusted.QBM**.

6. On January 20, 2017, the account receivable of Delphi Clothiers, amounting to $930, is determined to be uncollectible and is to be written off. Journalize and post this transaction in the general journal. (*Hint:* On the Make General Journal Entries window, uncheck Adjusting Entry.)

7. On November 26, 2017, the attorneys for Montana turned over a check for $930 that they obtained from Delphi Clothiers in settlement of its account, which had been written off on January 20. The money had already been recorded as a deposit. Journalize and post the general journal entry to reverse the write off.

8. Print the December 31, 2016 through November 26, 2017 journal.

9. Back up your data. The suggested file name is **Problem 15.1A.QBM**.

10. **Analyze:** When the financial statements are prepared for the year ended December 31, 2016, what net accounts receivable should be reported? Use a blank piece of paper or the *Working Papers* to complete the analysis question.

GETTING STARTED: Problem 15.2A

Follow these steps to start QuickBooks and restore the Problem 15.2A.Lucero Company.QBM file.

Instructions:

1. Start QuickBooks.
2. If the menu bar shows a company name, click File; Open or Restore Company.
3. The Open or Restore Company window appears. Select Restore a portable file.
4. Click [Next]. The Open Portable Company File window appears. In the Look in field, go to the appropriate location for the Problem 15.2A.Lucero Company.QBM file. Click on the file to highlight it. Click [Open]. (*Hint:* You can also double-click on the file name.)
5. The Open or Restore Company window appears. Click [Next].
6. The Save Company File as window appears. Accept the default file name or change it slightly. Click [Save]. When Lucero Company - QuickBooks Accountant 2014 appears, the file is restored.
7. Continue with the next section "My Company."

My Company

Before recording transactions for the Lucero Company, look at the My Company information included on the Problem 15.2A.Lucero Company.QBM file.

1. From the Icon Bar, select [My Company]. (*Or,* from the menu bar, select Company; My Company.) The My Company window appears.

2. To add your name to the Company Name field, click [icon]. Close the My Company window.

The schedule of accounts receivable by age shown below was prepared for the Lucero Company at the end of the firm's fiscal year on December 31, 2016.

			Past Due--Days		
Lucero Company					
Schedule of Accounts Receivable by Age					
December 31, 2016					
Account	**Balance**	**Current**	**1-30**	**31-60**	**Over 60**
Adson, Paul	850.00	850.00			
Allen, Alfred	1,000.00		700.00	300.00	
Ash, John	516.00				516.00
Bae, John	260.00	260.00			
Barker, Kelsie	144.00	94.00	50.00		
Bentley, Maggie	560.00	220.00	250.00	90.00	
Blair, Herman	116.00			74.00	42.00
(All other accts.)	47,054.00	39,576.00	5,000.00	1,536.00	942.00
Totals	50,500.00	41,000.00	6,000.00	2,000.00	1,500.00

Required:

1. Restore the Problem 15.2A.Lucero Company.QBM file.
2. Use a blank piece of paper or the *Working Papers* to compute the estimated uncollectible accounts at the end of the year using the following rates:

Current	2%
1-30 days past due	4%
31-60 days past due	10%
Over 60 days past due	30%

3. As of December 31, 2016, there is a credit balance of $308 in Allowance for Doubtful Accounts. Compute the amount of the adjustment for uncollectible accounts expense that must be made as part of the adjusting entries.

4. Journalize and post in the general journal, the adjustment for the estimated losses. Use Uncollectible Accounts Expense and Allowance for Doubtful Accounts.

5. On May 10, 2017, the $516 account receivable of John Ash was recognized as uncollectible. Journal and post this entry.

6. On June 12, 2017, a check for $300 was received from Zeke Martin to apply to his account which had been written off on November 8, 2016, as uncollectible. Record the reversal of the previous write-off in the general journal. (*Hint:* Record the payment of $300 from Zeke Martin. The transaction requires two entries: 1) Record reversing entry. 2) Record customer payment on the Receive Payments/Customer Payment window.)

7. Print the December 31, 2016 through June 12, 2017 journal.

8. Back up. The suggested file name is **Problem 15.2A.June 2017.QBM**.

9. Restore the Problem 15.2A.Lucero Company.QBM file. (*Hint:* If necessary change the company name slightly; for example, use 15.2ALucero Company.QBW.)

10. Suppose that instead of aging the accounts receivable, the company estimated the uncollectible accounts to be 2 percent of the total accounts receivable on December 31, 2016. Journalize and post the general journal entry to record the adjustment for estimated losses from uncollectible accounts. Assume that Allowance for Doubtful Accounts has a credit balance of $308 before the adjusting entry.

11. Print the December 31, 2016 journal.

12. Print the December 31, 2016 trial balance. Account No. 116, Allowance for Doubtful Accounts, shows a balance of $1,010.

13. Back up. The suggested file name is **Problem 15.2A.December 2016.QBM**.

14. **Analyze:** What impact would the change in estimation method described in Instruction 10 have on the net income for fiscal 2016? Use a blank piece of paper or the *Working Papers* to complete the analysis question.

GETTING STARTED: Problem 15.4A

Follow these steps to start QuickBooks and restore the Problem 15.4A.Pullman Company.QBM file.

Instructions:

1. Start QuickBooks.
2. If the menu bar shows a company name, click File; Open or Restore Company.
3. The Open or Restore Company window appears. Select Restore a portable file.
4. Click [Next]. The Open Portable Company File window appears. In the Look in field, go to the appropriate location for the Problem 15.4A.Pullman Company.QBM file. Click on the file to highlight it. Click [Open]. (*Hint:* You can also double-click on the file name.)

5. The Open or Restore Company window appears. Click [Next] .
6. The Save Company File as window appears. Accept the default file name or change it slightly. Click [Save] . When Pullman Company - QuickBooks Accountant 2014 appears, the file is restored.
7. Continue with the next section "My Company."

My Company

Before recording transactions for the Pullman Company, look at the My Company information included on the Problem 15.4A.Pullman Company.QBM file.

1. From the Icon Bar, select [My Company] . (*Or,* from the menu bar, select Company; My Company.) The My Company window appears.

2. To add your name to the Company Name field, click [✎] . Close the My Company window.

Pullman Company records uncollectible accounts expense as they occur. Selected transactions for 2016 and 2017 are described below. The accounts involved in these transactions are Notes Receivable, Accounts Receivable, and Uncollectible Accounts Expense.

Required:

1. Restore the Problem 15.4A.Pullman Company.QBM file.
2. Journalize and post the 2016 and 2017 transactions in the general journal.

2016

Feb.	7	The $700 account receivable of Anne Baker is determined to be uncollectible and is to be written off.
May	16	Because of the death of Martha Falls, her account receivable of $1,100 is considered uncollectible and is to be written off.
July	2	Received $350 from Anne Baker in partial payment of her account, which had been written off on February 7. The cash obtained has already been recorded. There is doubt that the balance of Baker's account will be collected.
July	29	Received $350 from Anne Baker to complete payment of her account, which had been written off on February 7. The cash obtained has already been recorded.
Aug.	18	The $424 account receivable of David Nye is determined to be uncollectible and is to be written off.

2017

Sept. 28 Received $550 from the estate of Martha Falls as part of the settlement of affairs. This amount is applicable to the account receivable written off on May 16, 2016. The cash obtained has already been recorded.

3. Print the February 7, 2016 through September 28, 2017 journal.
4. Back up. The suggested file name is **Problem 15.4A.QBM**.
5. **Analyze:** Based on these transactions, what net uncollectible accounts expense was recorded for the year 2016? (*Hint:* Print a February 7, 2016 through August 18, 2016 trial balance.) Use a blank piece of paper or the *Working Papers* to complete the analysis question.

Chapter 16

Notes Payable and Notes Receivable

In Chapter 16 of *College Accounting, 14e*, there are two QuickBooks problems.

➤ Problem 16.2A Dennis Company: Recording transactions involving notes payable.
➤ Problem 16.5A Reliable Company: Recording the receipt, discounting, and payment of notes receivable.

Chapter 16's QuickBooks activities demonstrate how to:

• Restore two QuickBooks problem templates.
• Journalize and post transactions.
• Print the journal.
• Complete Problem 16.2A and Problem 16.5A.

GETTING STARTED: Problem 16.2A

Follow these steps to start QuickBooks and restore the Problem 16.2A.Dennis Company.QBM file.

Instructions:

1. Start QuickBooks.
2. If the menu bar shows a company name, click File; Open or Restore Company.
3. The Open or Restore Company window appears. Select Restore a portable file.
4. Click . [Next] The Open Portable Company File window appears. In the Look in field, go to the appropriate location for the Problem 16.2A.Dennis Company.QBM file. Click on the file to highlight it. Click [Open] . (*Hint:* You can also double-click on the file name.)
5. The Open or Restore Company window appears. Click [Next] .
6. The Save Company File as window appears. Accept the default file name or change it slightly. Click [Save] . When Dennis Company - QuickBooks Accountant 2014 appears, the file is restored.
7. Continue with the next section "My Company."

My Company

Before recording transactions for Dennis Company, look at the My Company information included on the Problem 16.2A.Dennis Company.QBM file.

1. From the Icon Bar, select [My Company]. (*Or,* from the menu bar, select Company; My Company.) The My Company window appears.

2. To add your name to the Company Name field, click [pencil icon]. Close the My Company window.

Required:

1. Restore the Problem 16.2A.Dennis Company file.
2. Journalize and post the notes payable transactions shown below.

   a. Issued a 6-month, 9 percent note for $85,000 to purchase two forklifts on May 14, 2016 (debit Warehouse Equipment).
   b. Discounted its own 180-day, noninterest-bearing note with a principal amount of $39,000 at the Nelson Bank and Trust on May 28, 2016. The bank charged a discount rate of 10 percent.
   c. Paid the May 14 note on its due date.
   d. Paid the note discounted on May 28 on its due date.

3. Print the May 14 through November 24, 2016 journal.
4. Back up your data. The suggested file name is **Problem 16.2A.QBM**.
5. **Analyze:** What is the total interest expense for the year as a result of these transactions? Use a blank piece of paper or the *Working Papers* to complete the analysis question.

GETTING STARTED: Problem 16.5A

Follow these steps to start QuickBooks and restore the Problem 16.5A.Reliable Company.QBM file.

Instructions:

1. Start QuickBooks.
2. If the menu bar shows a company name, click File; Open or Restore Company.
3. The Open or Restore Company window appears. Select Restore a portable file.

4. Click [Next]. The Open Portable Company File window appears. In the Look in field, go to the appropriate location for the Problem 16.5A.Reliable Company.QBM file. Click on the file to highlight it. Click [Open]. (*Hint:* You can also double-click on the file name.)

5. The Open or Restore Company window appears. Click [Next].

6. The Save Company File as window appears. Accept the default file name or change it slightly. Click [Save]. When Reliable Company - QuickBooks Accountant 2014 appears, the file is restored.

7. Continue with the next section "My Company."

My Company

Before recording transactions for the Reliable Company, look at the My Company information included on the Problem 16.5A.Reliable Company.QBM file.

1. From the Icon Bar, select [My Company]. (Or, from the menu bar, select Company; My Company.) The My Company window appears.

2. To add your name to the Company Name field, click [pencil icon]. Close the My Company window.

Required:

1. Restore the Problem 16.5A.Reliable Company file.
2. Journalize and post the transactions shown below.

   a. On May 16, 2016, Reliable Company received a 90-day, 8 percent, $9,800 interest-bearing note from White Company in settlement of White's past-due account.
   b. On June 30, Reliable discounted this note at Fargo Bank and Trust. The bank charged a discount rate of 13 percent.
   c. On August 15, Reliable received a notice that White had paid the note and the interest on the due date.

3. Print the May 16 through August 14, 2016 journal.
4. Back up your data. The suggested file name is **Problem 16.5A.QBM**.
5. **Analyze:** If the company prepared a balance sheet on July 31, 2016, how should Notes Receivable-Discounted be presented on the statement? Use a blank piece of paper or the *Working Papers* to complete the analysis question.

Chapter 19

Accounting for Partnerships

In Chapter 19 of *College Accounting, 14e*, there are three QuickBooks problems.

➤ Problem 19.2A Oatis and Thomas Angler's Outpost: Accounting for formation of a partnership
➤ Problem 19.4A Larry's Antiques: Computing and recording the division of net income or loss between partners; preparing a statement of partners' equities.
➤ Problem 19.5A Adams Pharmacy: Accounting for revaluation of assets and liabilities of a partnership, investment of a new partner, and withdrawal of a partner.

Chapter 19's QuickBooks activities demonstrate how to:

- Restore three QuickBooks problem templates.
- Journalize and post transactions.
- Print the journal.
- Print the balance sheet.
- Complete Problem 19.2A, Problem 19.4A, and Problem 19.5A.

GETTING STARTED: Problem 19.2A

Follow these steps to start QuickBooks and restore the Problem 19.2A.Oatis and Thomas Angler's Outpost.QBM file.

Instructions:

1. Start QuickBooks.
2. If the menu bar shows a company name, click File; Open or Restore Company.
3. The Open or Restore Company window appears. Select Restore a portable file.
4. Click [Next]. The Open Portable Company File window appears. In the Look in field, go to the appropriate location for the Problem 19.2A.Oatis and Thomas Angler's Outpost.QBM file. Click on the file to highlight it. Click [Open]. (*Hint:* You can also double-click on the file name.)
5. The Open or Restore Company window appears. Click [Next].

6. The Save Company File as window appears. Accept the default file name or change it slightly. Click [Save]. When Oatis and Thomas Angler's Outpost - QuickBooks Accountant 2014 appears, the file is restored.

7. Continue with the next section "My Company."

My Company

Before recording transactions for the Oatis and Thomas Angler's Outpost, look at the My Company information included on the Problem 19.2A.Oatis and Thomas Angler's Outpost.QBM file.

1. From the Icon Bar, select [My Company]. (*Or,* from the menu bar, select Company; My Company.) The My Company window appears.

2. To add your name to the Company Name field, click [edit icon]. Close the My Company window.

Terry Oatis operates a small shop that sells fishing equipment. His postclosing trial balance on December 31, 2016 is shown below.

<table>
<tr><td colspan="3" align="center">**Oatis Tackle Center**
Postclosing Trial Balance
December 31, 2016</td></tr>
<tr><td align="center">Account Name</td><td align="center">Debit</td><td align="center">Credit</td></tr>
<tr><td>Cash</td><td align="center">4,750.00</td><td></td></tr>
<tr><td>Accounts Receivable</td><td align="center">16,400.00</td><td></td></tr>
<tr><td>Allowance for Doubtful Accounts</td><td></td><td align="center">2,500.00</td></tr>
<tr><td>Merchandise Inventory</td><td align="center">45,000.00</td><td></td></tr>
<tr><td>Furniture and Equipment</td><td align="center">29,100.00</td><td></td></tr>
<tr><td>Accumulated Depreciation</td><td></td><td align="center">23,000.00</td></tr>
<tr><td>Accounts Payable</td><td></td><td align="center">4,000.00</td></tr>
<tr><td>Capital</td><td></td><td align="center">65,750.00</td></tr>
<tr><td>Totals</td><td align="center">95,250.00</td><td align="center">95,250.00</td></tr>
</table>

Oatis plans to enter into a partnership with Carmen Thomas effective January 1, 2017. Profits and losses will be shared equally. Oatis is to transfer all assets and liabilities of his store to the partnership after revaluation as agreed. Thomas will invest cash equal to Oatis's investment after revaluation. The agreed values are Accounts Receivable (net) $14,500; Merchandise Inventory, $49,900; and Furniture and Equipment, $12,300. The partnership will operate as Oatis and Thomas Angler's Outpost.

Required:

1. Restore the Problem 19.2A.Oatis and Thomas Angler's Outpost.QBM file.
2. Journalize and post the following general journal entries.

    a. The receipt of Oatis's investment of assets and liabilities by the partnership.
    b. The receipt of Thomas's investment of cash.

3. Print the January 1, 2017 journal.
4. Print the 1/1/2017 balance sheet.
5. Back up. The suggested file name is **Problem 19.2A.QBM**.
6. **Analyze:** By what net amount were the net assets of Oatis's Tackle Center adjusted before they were transferred to the partnership? Use a blank piece of paper or the *Working Papers* to complete the analysis question.

GETTING STARTED: Problem 19.4A

Follow these steps to start QuickBooks and restore the Problem 19.4A.Larry's Antiques.QBM file.

Instructions:

1. Start QuickBooks.
2. If the menu bar shows a company name, click File; Open or Restore Company.
3. The Open or Restore Company window appears. Select Restore a portable file.
4. Click [Next]. The Open Portable Company File window appears. In the Look in field, go to the appropriate location for the Problem 19.4A.Larry's Antiques.QBM file. Click on the file to highlight it. Click [Open]. (*Hint:* You can also double-click on the file name.)
5. The Open or Restore Company window appears. Click [Next].
6. The Save Company File as window appears. Accept the default file name or change it slightly. Click [Save]. When Larry's Antiques - QuickBooks Accountant 2014 appears, the file is restored.
7. Continue with the next section "My Company."

My Company

Before recording transactions for Larry's Antiques, look at the My Company information included on the Problem 19.4A.Larry's Antiques.QBM file.

---

1. From the Icon Bar, select **My Company**. (*Or,* from the menu bar, select Company; My Company.) The My Company window appears.

2. To add your name to the Company Name field, click [pencil icon]. Close the My Company window.

Larry Watson and Larry Lewis own Larry's Antiques. Their partnership agreement provides for annual salary allowances of $100,000 for Watson and $90,000 for Lewis, and interest of 10 percent on each partner's invested capital at the beginning of the year. The remainder of the net income or loss is to be distributed 50 percent to Watson and 50 percent to Lewis. The partners withdraw their salary allowances monthly. On January 1, 2016, the capital account balances were Watson, $500,000, and Lewis, $460,000. On December 15, 2016, Lewis made a permanent withdrawal of $110,000. The net income for 2016 was $420,000.

Required:

1. Restore the Problem 19.4A.Larry's Antiques.QBM file.
2. On December 15, 2016, journalize and post the permanent withdrawal by Lewis.
3. On December 31, 2016, journalize and post the following general journal entries.

   a. Journalize and post the salary allowances for the year.
   b. Journalize and post the interest allowances for the year.
   c. Journalize and post the division of the balance of net income.
   d. Close the drawing accounts into the capital accounts, assuming that Watson and Lewis have withdrawn their full salary allowances.

4. On a blank piece of paper or in the *Working Papers*, prepare a schedule showing the division of net income to the partners as it would appear on the income statement for 2016.
5. On a blank piece of paper or in the *Working Papers*, prepare a statement of partners' equities showing the changes that took place in the partners' capital accounts during 2016.
6. Print the December 15 through 31, 2016 journal.
7. Back up. The suggested file name is **Problem 19.4A.QBM**.
8. **Analyze:** By what percentage did Watson's capital account increase in the fiscal year 2016? Use a blank piece of paper or the *Working Papers* to complete the analysis question.

GETTING STARTED: Problem 19.5A

Follow these steps to start QuickBooks and restore the Problem 19.5A.Adams Pharmacy.QBM file.

Instructions:

1. Start QuickBooks.
2. If the menu bar shows a company name, click File; Open or Restore Company.
3. The Open or Restore Company window appears. Select Restore a portable file.

4. Click **Next**. The Open Portable Company File window appears. In the Look in field, go to the appropriate location for the Problem 19.5A.Adams Pharmacy.QBM file. Click on the file to highlight it. Click **Open**. (*Hint:* You can also double-click on the file name.)

5. The Open or Restore Company window appears. Click **Next**.
6. The Save Company File as window appears. Accept the default file name or change it slightly. Click **Save**. When Adams Pharmacy - QuickBooks Accountant 2014 appears, the file is restored.
7. Continue with the next section "My Company."

My Company

Before recording transactions for the Adams Pharmacy, look at the My Company information included on the Problem 19.5A.Adams Pharmacy.QBM file.

1. From the Icon Bar, select **My Company**. (*Or,* from the menu bar, select Company; My Company.) The My Company window appears.

2. To add your name to the Company Name field, click [pencil icon]. Close the My Company window.

The balance sheet of Adams Pharmacy after the revenue, expense, and partners' drawing accounts have been closed on December 31, 2016, follows. These balances are included on the Problem 19.5A.Adams Pharmacy.QBM file. Display the 12/31/2016 balance sheet and compare it to the one shown on page 106.

Adams Pharmacy
Balance Sheet
As of December 31, 2016

	⋄ Dec 31, 16 ⋄
▼ ASSETS	
▼ Current Assets	
▼ Checking/Savings	
101 · Cash	▶ 83,400.00 ◀
Total Checking/Savings	83,400.00
▼ Other Current Assets	
112 · Accounts Receivable	17,000.00
120 · Merchandise Inventory	435,000.00
Total Other Current Assets	452,000.00
Total Current Assets	535,400.00
▼ Fixed Assets	
125 · Equipment	174,000.00
127 · Accumulated Depr.-Equipment	-101,000.00
129 · Building	420,000.00
131 · Accumulated Depr.-Building	-330,000.00
133 · Land	50,000.00
Total Fixed Assets	213,000.00
TOTAL ASSETS	**748,400.00**
▼ LIABILITIES & EQUITY	
▼ Liabilities	
▼ Current Liabilities	
▼ Other Current Liabilities	
201 · Accounts Payable	415,200.00
205 · Taxes Payable	23,200.00
Total Other Current Liabilities	438,400.00
Total Current Liabilities	438,400.00
Total Liabilities	438,400.00
▼ Equity	
301 · Larry Adams, Capital	170,000.00
303 · Hazel Adams, Capital	70,000.00
305 · Isiah Adams, Capital	70,000.00
Total Equity	310,000.00
TOTAL LIABILITIES & EQUITY	**748,400.00**

On December 31, 2016, Larry Adams, Hazel Adams, and Isiah Adams agree to admit Vickie Neal to the partnership. The partnership agreement provides that, in case of dissolution of the partnership, all assets and liabilities should be revalued. Profits and losses are shared in the ratio of 50:25:25, to Larry, Hazel, and Isiah, respectively. The agreed upon values of the assets are as follows:

Accounts receivable	$ 15,000
Merchandise inventory	408,400
Equipment	73,000
Building	139,000
Land	103,000

All liabilities are properly recorded.

Required:

1. Restore the Problem 19.5A.Adams Pharmacy.QBM file.
2. Journalize and post the general journal entries to record revaluation of the assets. (*Hint*: After completing each transaction shown in steps 2-6, look at the partners' general ledger account balances. This will help determine the appropriate entries. You may also want to backup after each transaction is completed.)
3. Journalize and post the entry (or entries) to record Vickie Neal's investment of $120,000, assuming that she is to receive capital equal to the amount invested.
4. Journalize and post the entry (or entries) to record Vickie Neal's investment of $120,000, assuming that she is to receive one-fifth of the capital of the partnership.
5. Journalize and post the entry (or entries) to record Vickie Neal's investment of $120,000, assuming that she is to receive one-third of the capital of the partnership.
6. Assume that after the revaluation had been recorded, the existing partners and Vickie Neal decided that their previous agreement should be canceled and that Vickie Neal should not become a partner. Instead, the partners agreed that Hazel Adams would withdraw from the partnership and be paid cash by the partnership.

   a. Journalize and post the general journal entry to record the payment to Hazel Adams if she is paid an amount equal to her capital account balance after the revaluation.
   b. Journalize and post the entry to record the payment to Hazel Adams if she is paid an amount equal to $15,000 less than her capital account balance after revaluation.
   c. Journalize and post the entry to record the payment to Hazel Adams if she is paid an amount equal to $12,600 more than her capital account balance after revaluation.

7. Print the December 31, 2016 journal.
8. Back up. The suggested file name is **Problem 19.5A.QBM**.
9. **Analyze:** Assume that only items 2 and 4 have been recorded in the records of the partnership. What is the balance of Isiah Adams's capital account at January 1, 2017? Use a blank piece of paper or the *Working Papers* to complete the analysis question.

Chapter 20

Corporations: Formation and Capital Stock Transactions

In Chapter 20 of *College Accounting, 14e*, there are two QuickBooks problems.

- ➢ Problem 20.4A Denzel Corporation: Issuing stock at par and no-par value, recording organization costs, and preparing a balance sheet.
- ➢ Problem 20.5A Jaguar Corporation: Issuing stock at par and at premium, preparing Stockholders' Equity section of balance sheet, and recording stock subscriptions.

Chapter 20's QuickBooks activities demonstrate how to:

- Restore two QuickBooks problem templates.
- Journalize and post transactions.
- Print the journal.
- Print the balance sheet.
- Complete Problem 20.4A and Problem 20.5A.

GETTING STARTED: Problem 20.4A

Follow these steps to start QuickBooks and restore the Problem 20.4A.Denzel Corporation.QBM file.

Instructions:

1. Start QuickBooks.
2. If the menu bar shows a company name, click File; Open or Restore Company.
3. The Open or Restore Company window appears. Select Restore a portable file.
4. Click [Next]. The Open Portable Company File window appears. In the Look in field, go to the appropriate location for the Problem 20.4A.Denzel

   Corporation.QBM file. Click on the file to highlight it. Click [Open]. (*Hint:* You can also double-click on the file name.)
5. The Open or Restore Company window appears. Click [Next].
6. The Save Company File as window appears. Accept the default file name or change it

   slightly. Click [Save]. When Denzel Corporation - QuickBooks Accountant 2014 appears, the file is restored.
7. Continue with the next section "My Company."

My Company

Before recording transactions for the Denzel Corporation, look at the My Company information included on the Problem 20.4A.Denzel Corporation.QBM file.

1. From the Icon Bar, select [My Company]. (*Or,* from the menu bar, select Company; My Company.) The My Company window appears.

2. To add your name to the Company Name field, click [pencil icon]. Close the My Company window.

Denzel Corporation, a new corporation, took over the assets and liabilities of Delta Art on January 2, 2016. The assets and liabilities, after appropriate revaluation by Denzel, are as follows.

Cash	$ 51,500
Accounts Receivable	372,000
Allowance for Doubtful Accounts	(13,600)
Merchandise Inventory	700,000
Accounts Payable	(385,000)
Accrued Expenses Payable	(21,800)

The corporation is authorized to issue 600,000 shares of $15 par-value common stock and 400,000 shares of $10 par-value preferred stock. The preferred stock bears a stated yearly dividend rate of $1 per share. The transactions that follow were entered into at the time the corporation was formed.

Required:

1. Restore the Problem 20.4A.Denzel Corporation.QBM file. Prepare the opening balance sheet as of January 2, 2016, for Denzel Corporation.
2. Journalize and post the transactions shown below in the general journal. (*Hint:* Refer to the asset and liability account balances shown above.)

Jan.	2	The corporation issued 46,000 shares of common stock to James Denzel for his equity in the sole proprietorship business, and the corporation took over Denzel's assets and liabilities.
	2	Issued 3,000 shares of preferred stock at par to Harriet Denzel, James' wife, for cash.
	2	Issued 9,000 shares of common stock to Carol Kennedy. She paid $135,000 in cash for the stock.
	2	Issued 5,000 shares of preferred stock to James Walker. He paid $50,000 in cash for the stock.

3. Print the January 2, 2016 journal.
4. Print the January 2, 2016 balance sheet.
5. Back up your data. The suggested file name is **Problem 20.4A.QBM**.
6. **Analyze:** What is the current ratio for the corporation at January 2, 2016? Use a blank piece of paper or the *Working Papers* to complete the analysis question.

GETTING STARTED: Problem 20.5A

Follow these steps to start QuickBooks and restore the Problem 20.5A.Jaguar Corporation.QBM file.

Instructions:

1. Start QuickBooks.
2. If the menu bar shows a company name, click File; Open or Restore Company.
3. The Open or Restore Company window appears. Select Restore a portable file.
4. Click Next. The Open Portable Company File window appears. In the Look in field, go to the appropriate location for the Problem 20.5A.Jaguar Corporation.QBM file. Click on the file to highlight it. Click Open. (*Hint:* You can also double-click on the file name.)
5. The Open or Restore Company window appears. Click Next.
6. The Save Company File as window appears. Accept the default file name or change it slightly. Click Save. When Jaguar Corporation - QuickBooks Accountant 2014 appears, the file is restored.
7. Continue with the next section "My Company."

My Company

Before recording transactions for the Jaguar Corporation, look at the My Company information included on the Problem 20.5A.Jaguar Corporation.QBM file.

1. From the Icon Bar, select My Company. (*Or,* from the menu bar, select Company; My Company.) The My Company window appears.

2. To add your name to the Company Name field, click . Close the My Company window.

Jaguar Corporation was organized on March 1, 2016, to operate a delivery service. The firm is authorized to issue 75,000 shares of no-par-value common stock with a stated value of $100 per share and 30,000 shares of $100 par-value, 8 percent preferred stock that is nonparticipating and noncumulative. Selected transactions that took place during March 2016 follow.

You may want to review the chart of accounts included on the Problem 20.5A.Jaguar Corporaiton.QBM file to review the general ledger accounts used to complete this problem.

Date	Transactions
March 1	The corporation received its charter. (Make a memorandum entry.)
1	Issued 650 shares of common stock for cash at $100 per share to Jerri Harris.
3	Issued 400 shares of preferred stock for cash at par value to Gloria Amos.
5	Issued 400 shares of common stock for cash at $107 to Carolyn Reed.
5	Received a subscription for 450 shares of common stock at $106 per share from Joan Patterson, payable in two installments due in 10 and 20 days.
14	Received a subscription for 300 shares of preferred stock at $109 per share from Robert Tolliver, payable in two installments due in 15 and 30 days.
20	Received payment of a stock subscription installment due from Joan Patterson (one-half of the purchase price—see March 5 transaction).
29	Received payment of a stock subscription installment due from Robert Tolliver (one-half the purchase price—see March 14 transaction).
30	Received the balance due on the stock subscription of March 5 from Joan Patterson; issued the stock.

Required:

1. Restore the Problem 20.5A.Jaguar Corporation.QBM file.
2. For the March 1, 2016 memorandum entry use a blank piece of paper or the *Working Papers*.
3. Journalize and post the transactions shown above.
4. Print the March 1-30, 2016 journal.
5. Print the March 1-30, 2016 general ledger.
6. To prepare a stockholders' equity section, print the March 31, 2016 balance sheet. (*Hint:* The Equity section of QuickBooks' balance sheet can be substituted for the Stockholders' Equity section.)
7. Back up your data. The suggested file name is **Problem 20.5A.QBM**.
8. **Analyze:** What percentage of total stockholders' equity is held by common stockholders? Use a blank piece of paper or the *Working Papers* to complete the analysis question.

Chapter 21

Corporate Earnings and Capital Transactions

In Chapter 21 of *College Accounting, 14e*, there are three QuickBooks problems.

- ➤ Problem 21.1A Divad Corporation: Recording federal income tax transactions and cash dividend transactions.
- ➤ Problem 21.3A Solomon Corporation: Recording cash dividends, stock dividends, and appropriation of retained earnings; preparing statement of retained earnings.
- ➤ Problem 21.4A Willy Corporation: Recording cash dividends, stock splits, appropriations of retained earnings, and donated assets; preparing the Stockholders' Equity section of the balance sheet.

Chapter 21's QuickBooks activities demonstrate how to:

- Restore three QuickBooks problem templates.
- Journalize and post transactions.
- Print the journal.
- Print the general ledger.
- Complete Problem 21.1A, Problem 21.3A, and Problem 21.4A.

GETTING STARTED: Problem 21.1A

Follow these steps to start QuickBooks and restore the Problem 21.1A.Divad Corporation.QBM file.

Instructions:

1. Start QuickBooks.
2. If the menu bar shows a company name, click File; Open or Restore Company.
3. The Open or Restore Company window appears. Select Restore a portable file.
4. Click [Next]. The Open Portable Company File window appears. In the Look in field, go to the appropriate location for the Problem 21.1A.Divad Corporation.QBM file. Click on the file to highlight it. Click [Open]. (*Hint:* You can also double-click on the file name.)
5. The Open or Restore Company window appears. Click [Next].

6. The Save Company File as window appears. Accept the default file name or change it slightly. Click [Save]. When Divad Corporation - QuickBooks Accountant 2014 appears, the file is restored.

7. Continue with the next section "My Company."

My Company

Before recording transactions for the Divad Corporation, look at the My Company information included on the Problem 21.1A.Divad Corporation.QBM file.

1. From the Icon Bar, select [My Company]. (*Or,* from the menu bar, select Company; My Company.) The My Company window appears.

2. To add your name to the Company Name field, click [ ]. Close the My Company window.

Selected transactions of Divad Corporation during 2016 follow. Record them in the general journal.

Date	*Transactions*
Mar. 15	Filed the federal income tax return for 2015. The total tax for the year was $136,750. During 2015, quarterly deposits of estimated tax totaling $130,000 had been made. The additional tax of $6,750 was paid with the return. On December 31, 2015, the accountant had estimated the total tax for 2015 to be $134,600 and had recorded a liability of $4,600 for federal income tax payable.
Apr. 15	Paid first quarterly installment of $42,000 on 2016 estimated federal income tax.
May 3	Declared dividend of $0.20 per share on the 50,000 shares of common stock outstanding. The dividend is payable on June 2 to stockholders of record as of May 20, 2016.
June 2	Paid dividend declared on May 3.
15	Paid second quarterly installment of $42,000 on 2016 estimated federal income tax.
Sept. 15	Paid third quarterly installment of $42,000 on 2016 estimated federal income tax.
Nov. 2	Declared dividend of $0.20 per share on 50,000 shares of common stock outstanding. The dividend is payable on December 2 to holders of record on November 20.
Dec. 2	Paid dividend declared on November 2.
15	Paid fourth quarterly installment of $42,000 on 2016 estimated income tax.
31	Total income tax for 2016 was $169,040. Record as an adjustment the difference between this amount and the total quarterly deposits.

Required:

1. Restore the Problem 21.1A.Divad Corporation.QBM file.
2. Journalize and post the transactions shown on page 114.
3. Print the March 15 to December 31, 2016 journal.
4. Back up. The suggested file name is **Problem 21.1A.QBM**.
5. **Analyze:** What annual per share dividend was paid to common stockholders in 2016?

GETTING STARTED: Problem 21.3A

Follow these steps to start QuickBooks and restore the Problem 21.3A.Solomon Corporation.QBM files.

Instructions:

1. Start QuickBooks.
2. If the menu bar shows a company name, click File; Open or Restore Company.
3. The Open or Restore Company window appears. Select Restore a portable file.
4. Click [Next]. The Open Portable Company File window appears. In the Look in field, go to the appropriate location for the Problem 21.3A.Solomon Corporation.QBM file. Click on the file to highlight it. Click [Open]. (*Hint:* You can also double-click on the file name.)
5. The Open or Restore Company window appears. Click [Next].
6. The Save Company File as window appears. Accept the default file name or change it slightly. Click [Save]. When Solomon Corporation - QuickBooks Accountant 2014 appears, the file is restored.
7. Continue with the next section "My Company."

My Company

Before recording transactions for the Solomon Corporation, look at the My Company information included on the Problem 21.3A.Solomon Corporation.QBM file.

1. From the Icon Bar, select [My Company]. (*Or,* from the menu bar, select Company; My Company.) The My Company window appears.

2. To add your name to the Company Name field, click [ ]. Close the My Company window.

The stockholders' equity accounts of Solomon Corporation on January 1, 2016, contained the following balances.

Preferred Stock (10%, $50 par value, 4,000 shares authorized)			
Issued and Outstanding, 1,700 shares		$85,000	
Paid-in Capital in Excess of Par Value-Preferred		1,700	$ 86,700
Common Stock ($20 par value, 30,000 shares authorized)			
Issued and Outstanding, 15,000 shares			300,000
Retained Earnings			207,200
Total Stockholders' Equity			593,900

Transaction affecting stockholders' equity during 2016 follow.

Date	Transactions
June 15	Declared a semiannual dividend of 5 percent on preferred stock, payable on July 15 to stockholders of record on June 30.
July 15	Paid the dividend on preferred stock.
Dec. 15	Declared a semiannual dividend of 5 percent on preferred stock, payable on January 15, 2017, to stockholders of record on December 31, 2016, and a cash dividend of $4 per share on common stock, payable on January 15, 2017, to stockholders of record on December 31, 2016. Make separate entries.
15	Declared a 10 percent common stock dividend to common stockholders of record on December 31, 2016. The new shares are to be issued on January 15, 2017. A fair value price of $25 per share is expected for the new shares of common stock.
31	Created an "appropriation of retained earnings for contingencies" of $60,000 because of the poor economic outlook.
31	The Income Summary account contained a debit balance of $20,000. The board had anticipated a net loss for the year and no quarterly deposits of estimated income taxes were made, so income taxes may be ignored.

Required:

1. Restore the Problem 21.3A.Solomon Corporation.QBM file.
2. The Problem 21.3A.Solomon Corporation.QBM file includes a June 1, 2016 beginning balance in the Retained Earnings account. To see the Retained Earnings beginning balance, display the June 1, 2016 general ledger. Account No. 381, Retained Earnings, is shown below.

381 · Retained Earnings					0.00
General Journal	06/01/2016	1	101 · Cash		207,200.00	-207,200.00
Total 381 · Retained Earnings				0.00	207,200.00	-207,200.00

3. Journalize and post the transactions shown above.

4. Print the June 15 to December 31, 2016 journal.
5. Print the June 1 to December 31, 2016 general ledger.
6. Use a blank piece of paper or the *Working Papers* to prepare a statement of retained earnings or the year 2016.
7. Back up. The suggested file name is **Problem 21.3A.QBM**.
8. **Analyze:** If Solomon Corporation had not declared cash or stock dividends for common stockholders, what balance would be found in the unappropriated Retained Earnings account at December 31, 2016? Use a blank piece of paper or the *Working Papers* to complete the analysis question.

GETTING STARTED: Problem 21.4A

Follow these steps to start QuickBooks and restore the Problem 21.4A.Willy Corporation.QBM file.

1. Start QuickBooks.
2. If the menu bar shows a company name, click File; Open or Restore Company.
3. The Open or Restore Company window appears. Select Restore a portable file.
4. Click [Next]. The Open Portable Company File window appears. In the Look in field, go to the appropriate location for the Problem 21.4A.Willy Corporation.QBM file. Click on the file to highlight it. Click [Open]. (*Hint:* You can also double-click on the file name.)
5. The Open or Restore Company window appears. Click [Next].
6. The Save Company File as window appears. Accept the default file name or change it slightly. Click [Save]. When Willy Corporation - QuickBooks Accountant 2014 appears, the file is restored.
7. Continue with the next section "My Company."

My Company

Before recording transactions for the Willy Corporation, look at the My Company information included on the Problem 21.4A.Willy Corporation.QBM file.

1. From the Icon Bar, select [My Company]. (*Or,* from the menu bar, select Company; My Company.) The My Company window appears.

2. To add your name to the Company Name field, click [✎]. Close the My Company window.

The Stockholders' Equity section of the balance sheet of Willy Corporation on January 1, 2016, is shown below; selected transaction for the year follow.

Preferred Stock (10% cumulative, $10 par value, 200,000 shares authorized)
 Issued and Outstanding, 9,000 Shares $90,000
 Paid-in Capital in Excess of Par Value   9,000 $ 99,000
Common Stock (no-par value, $50 stated value,
 300,000 shares authorized)
 Issued and Outstanding, 3,000 Shares   150,000
 Paid-in Capital in Excess of Stated Value   6,000   156,000
Total Paid-in Capital   255,000
Retained Earnings   140,000
 Total Stockholders' Equity $395,000

Date	Transactions
Feb. 15	Repurchased 4,100 shares of the outstanding preferred stock for $45,100 in cash. The stock is to be held as treasury stock. State law requires that an amount of retained earnings equal to the cost of treasury stock held must be appropriated. Record the purchase and the appropriation of retained earnings.
Mar. 4	Declared a 2-for-1 stock split of common stock. Each shareholder will own twice as many shares as originally owned. Stated value is reduced to $25 per share. Date of record is March 15. Date of issue of new shares is April 1.
Apr. 1	Issued new shares called for by split.
June 17	Declared semiannual dividend of 5 percent on preferred stock, to be paid on July 12 to holders of record on June 30.
July 12	Paid cash dividend on preferred stock.
Sept. 25	Purchased 600 shares of outstanding preferred stock at $10 per share to be held as treasury stock. Record appropriated retained earnings equal to cost of the treasury stock.
Dec. 15	Declared semiannual cash dividend of 5 percent on preferred stock to be paid on January 12 to holders of record on December 30.
15	Declared cash dividend of $1.40 per share on common stock to be paid on January 12 to holders of record on December 30.
15	Accepted title to a tract of land with a fair market value of $160,000 from the City of Greenville. The tract is to be used as a building site for the corporation's new factory.
31	Had net income after taxes for the year of $80,000. Give the entry to close the Income Summary account

Required:

1. Restore the Problem 21.4A.Willy Corporation.QBM file.
2. Journalize and post the February 15 to December 31, 2016 transactions shown above. Use a blank piece of paper or the *Working Papers* for journal entries that require an explanation only. Date the memorandum entries appropriately.
3. Print the February 15 to December 31, 2016 journal.

4. Print the February 1, 2016 to December 31, 2016 general ledger.
5. Print the December 31, 2016 balance sheet. Refer to the Equity section for the total amount of stockholders' equity.
6. Back up. The suggested file name is **Problem 21.4A.QBM**.
7. **Analyze:** If Willy Corporation had not repurchased preferred stock to place in treasury, what total stockholders' equity would be reported on December 31, 2016? Use a blank piece of paper or the *Working Papers* to complete the analysis question.

Chapter

22   Long-Term Bonds

In Chapter 22 of *College Accounting, 14e,* there are three QuickBooks problems.

> ➤ Problem 22.1A Carlie Services Inc.: Issuing bonds; bond interest transactions.
> ➤ Problem 22.4A New Computer Technology, Inc.: Recording bond sinking fund transactions, retained earnings appropriated for bond retirement, and retirement of bonds.
> ➤ Mini-Practice Set 3 The Texas Company: Corporation Accounting Cycle.

Chapter 22's QuickBooks activities demonstrate how to:

- Restore three QuickBooks problem templates.
- Journalize and post transactions.
- Print the journal.
- Print the balance sheet.
- Complete Problem 22.1A, and Problem 22.4A, Mini-Practice Set 3.

GETTING STARTED: Problem 22.1A

Follow these steps to start QuickBooks and restore the Problem 22.1A.Carlie Services Inc.QBM file.

Instructions:

1. Start QuickBooks.
2. If the menu bar shows a company name, click File; Open or Restore Company.
3. The Open or Restore Company window appears. Select Restore a portable file.
4. Click [**Next**]. The Open Portable Company File window appears. In the Look in field, go to the appropriate location for the Problem 22.1A.Carlie Services Inc.QBM file. Click on the file to highlight it. Click [**Open**]. (*Hint:* You can also double-click on the file name.)
5. The Open or Restore Company window appears. Click .

---

6. The Save Company File as window appears. Accept the default file name or change it slightly. Click [Save]. When Carlie Services Inc. - QuickBooks Accountant 2014 appears, the file is restored.

7. Continue with the next section "My Company."

My Company

Before recording transactions for Carlie Services Inc., look at the My Company information included on the Problem 22.1A.Carlie Services Inc.QBM file.

1. From the Icon Bar, select [My Company]. (*Or,* from the menu bar, select Company; My Company.) The My Company window appears.

2. To add your name to the Company Name field, click [ ]. Close the My Company window.

The board of directors of Carlie Services Inc. authorized the issuance of $400,000 face value, 20-year, 7 percent bonds dated April 1, 2016, and maturing on April 1, 2036. Interest is payable semiannually on April 1 and October 1. Carlie uses the calendar year as its fiscal year. The bond transactions that occurred in 2016 and 2017 follow.

Date	Transactions for 2016
Apr. 1	Issued $300,000 of bonds at face value.
Oct. 1	Paid semiannual interest on the bonds issued.
Dec. 31	Recorded the adjusting entry for the accrued bond interest.
31	Closed the Bond Interest Expense account to the Income Summary account.

	Transactions for 2017
Jan. 1	Reversed the adjusting entry made on December 31, 2016.
Apr. 1	Issued $100,000 of bonds at face value.
1	Paid the interest for six months on the bonds previously issued.
Oct. 1	Paid the interest for six months on the outstanding bonds.
Dec. 31	Recorded the adjusting entry for the accrued bond interest.
31	Closed the Bond Interest Expense account to the Income Summary account.

Required:

1. Restore the Problem 22.1A.Carlie Services Inc.QBM file.
2. Journalize and post the April 1 to December 31, 2016 transactions. (Round to the nearest dollar.)

3. **Analyze:** Based on the transactions given, what is the balance in the Bonds Payable account on December 31, 2016? You can display the general ledger to check the bonds payable account balance. Use a blank piece of paper or the *Working Papers* to complete the analysis question.
4. Back up. The suggested file name is **Problem 22.1A.2016.QBM**.
5. Journalize and post the January 1 to December 31, 2017 transactions. (Round to the nearest dollar.)
6. Print the April 1, 2016 to December 31, 2017 journal.
7. Back up. The suggested file name is **Problem 22.1A.2017.QBM**.

GETTING STARTED: Problem 22.4A

Follow these steps to start QuickBooks and restore the Problem 22.4A.New Computer Technology, Inc.QBM file.

Instructions:

1. Start QuickBooks.
2. If the menu bar shows a company name, click File; Open or Restore Company.
3. The Open or Restore Company window appears. Select Restore a portable file.
4. Click [Next]. The Open Portable Company File window appears. In the Look in field, go to the appropriate location for the Problem 22.4A.New Computer Technology, Inc.QBM file. Click on the file to highlight it. Click [Open]. (*Hint:* You can also double-click on the file name.)
5. The Open or Restore Company window appears. Click [Next].
6. The Save Company File as window appears. Accept the default file name or change it slightly. Click [Save]. When New Computer Technology, Inc - QuickBooks Accountant 2014 appears, the file is restored.
7. Continue with the next section "My Company."

My Company

Before recording transactions for New Computer Technology, Inc. look at the My Company information included on the Problem 22.4A.New Computer Technology, Inc.QBM file.

1. From the Icon Bar, select [My Company]. (*Or,* from the menu bar, select Company; My Company.) The My Company window appears.

2. To add your name to the Company Name field, click [pencil icon]. Close the My Company window.

New Computer Technology, Inc. has outstanding $600,000 of its 10 percent bonds payable, dated January 1, 2016, and maturing on January 1, 2036, 20 years later. The corporation is required under the bond contract to transfer $30,000 to a sinking fund each year. The directors have also voted to restrict retained earnings by transferring $30,000 each year on January 1 over the life of the bond issue to a Retained Earnings Appropriated for Bond Retirement account.

Required:

In the steps that follow you are going to restore the Problem 22.4A.New Computer Technology, Inc.QBM two times.

1. Restore the Problem 22.4A.New Computer Technology, Inc.QBM file.
2. Journalize and post the general journal entries to record the January 1, 2016, issuance of bonds at face value, the establishment of the Bond Sinking Fund Investment account, and the appropriation of retained earnings.
3. Use a blank piece of paper or the *Working Papers* to show how the Bond Sinking Fund Investment account and the Retained Earnings Appropriated for Bond Retirement account would be presented on the balance sheet as of December 31, 2020. (Assume that the ending balance of the Bond Sinking Fund Investment was $150,000 and the Retained Earnings-Unappropriated account was $320,210.)
4. Print the January 1, 2016 journal.
5. Back up. The suggested file name is **Problem 22.4A.Face Value.QBM**.
6. Restore the Problem 22.4A.New Computer Technology, Inc.QBM. (*Hint:* If necessary, change the name slightly when restoring the .QBW company file; for example, use the problem number in the file name.)
7. Assuming that the Bond Sinking Fund Investment account had a balance of $600,000 on January 1, 2036, journalize and post the general journal entry to record the retirement of the bonds and remove the appropriation for retained earnings.
8. Print the January 1, 2036 journal.
9. Back up. The suggested file name is **Problem 22.4A.Bond Retirement.QBM**.
10. **Analyze:** What percentage of total retained earnings has been appropriated for bond retirement on December 31, 2020? Use a blank piece of paper or the *Working Papers* to complete the analysis question.

MINI-PRACTICE SET 3: CORPORATION ACCOUNTING CYCLE

This project will give you an opportunity to apply your knowledge of accounting principles and procedures to a corporation. You will handle the accounting work of The Texas Company for 2016.

The Chart of accounts and account balances of The Texas Company on January 1, 2016 are shown on the next page. The Texas Company *does not* use reversing entries.

The Texas Company
Chart of Accounts/Account Balances on January 1, 2016

Account No./Account Name	Debit	Credit
101 Cash	$176,000	
103 Accounts Receivable	170,000	
104 Allowance for Doubtful Accounts		$ 5,000
105 Subscriptions Rec.-Common Stock		
121 Interest Receivable		
131 Merchandise Inventory	150,000	
141 Land	85,000	
151 Buildings	225,000	
152 Accum. Depr.-Buildings		22,500
161 Furniture and Equipment	70,000	
162 Accum. Depr.-Furn. and Equip.		14,000
181 Organization Costs	6,000	
202 Accounts Payable		75,000
203 Interest Payable		2,500
205 Estimated Income Taxes Payable		17,000
206 Dividends Payable-Preferred Stock		
207 Dividends Payable-Common Stock		
211 10-year, 10% Bonds Payable		100,000
212 Premium on Bonds Payable		2,625
301 5% Preferred Stock ($100 par, 10,000 shares authorized)		100,000
302 Paid-In Capital in Excess of Par—Preferred Stock		10,000
303 Common Stock ($10 par, 100,000 shares authorized)		200,000
304 Paid in Capital in Excess of Par—Common Stock		25,000
305 Common Stock Subscribed		
306 Common Stock Dividend Distributable		
311 Retained Earnings Appropriated		100,000
312 Retained Earnings Unappropriated		208,375
343 Treasury Stock—Preferred		
399 Income Summary		
401 Sales		
501 Purchases		
601 Operating Expenses		
701 Interest Income		
711 Gain on Early Retirement of Bonds Payable		
751 Interest Expense		
753 Amortization of Organization Costs		
801 Income Tax Expense		
Totals	**$882,000**	**$882,000**

DATE		TRANSACTIONS FOR 2016
Jan.	5	Issued 1,000 shares of 5 percent $100 par preferred stock for $101 per share. (The corporation has been authorized to issue 10,000 shares of preferred stock.)
	15	Paid estimated income taxes of $17,000 accrued at the end of 2015.
Apr.	1	Paid semiannual bond interest on the 10-year, 10 percent bonds payable and amortized the premium for the period since December 31, 2015. (The interest and premium were recorded as of December 31, 2015; the entry was not reversed.) The bonds were issued on October 1, 2014, at a price of 103, and they mature on October 1, 2024. Use straight-line amortization.
July	1	The Texas Company's board of directors declared a cash dividend of $0.10 per share on the common stock. The dividend is payable on July 26 to stockholders of record as of July 15.
	26	Paid the cash dividend on the common stock.
Aug.	12	A purchaser of 600 shares of preferred stock issued on January 5 asked the corporation to repurchase the shares. The corporation repurchased the stock for $102 per share. The stock is to be held by the corporation until it can be resold to another purchaser.
Oct.	1	Paid the semiannual bond interest and recorded amortization of the bond premium.
Dec.	1	Because of its good cash position and current bond prices, the Texas Company repurchased and retired $20,000 par value of the 10 percent bonds that it has outstanding. The repurchase price was 98, plus accrued interest.
	15	The company's board of directors declared a cash dividend of $5 per share on the outstanding preferred stock. This dividend is payable on January 10 to stockholders of record as of December 31.
	15	The board of directors also declared a 10 percent stock dividend on the outstanding common stock. The new shares are to be distributed on January 10 to stockholders of record as of December 31. At the time the dividend was declared, the common stock had a fair market value of $15 per share.
	30	Received a subscription for 500 shares of The Texas Company's common stock at $12 per share from the company's president. Received cash equal to one-half the purchase price on the date of subscription. The balance of the purchase price is to be paid on January 15, 2017. (The subscriber will not be entitled to the stock dividend previously declared on the outstanding shares of common stock.)
	30	Because the management of Texas foresees the need to expand a warehouse the firm owns, the board of directors has restricted future dividend payments. Record the appropriation of $100,000 of retained earnings for plant expansion.

December 31, 2016 Summary Operating Transactions

Journalize and post the following summary operating transactions using December 31, 2016, as the date.

1. Total sales of merchandise for the year were $2,800,000. All sales were on credit.
2. Total collections on accounts receivable during the year were $2,810,000.
3. Total purchases of merchandise for the year were $1,880,000. All purchases were on credit.
4. Total operating expenses incurred during the year were $650,000. (Debit Operating Expenses and credit Accounts Payable.)
5. Total cash payments on accounts payable during the year were $2,335,000.
6. Total accounts receivable charged off as uncollectible during the year were $10,000. (The Texas Company uses the allowance method to record uncollectible accounts.)

Data for Year-End Adjustments

1. The balance of Allowance for Doubtful Accounts should be adjusted to equal 3 percent of the balance of Accounts Receivable. (Debit Operating Expenses.)
2. Depreciation on the buildings should be recorded. (Debit Operating Expenses.) The firm uses the straight-line method and an estimated life of 20 years to compute this adjustment.
3. Depreciation on furniture and equipment should be recorded. The firm uses the straight-line method and an estimated life of 10 years to compute this adjustment. (Debit Operating Expenses.)
4. Accrued interest on the outstanding bonds payable of The Texas Company should be recorded and the premium amortized.
5. The amortization of organization costs for the year should be recorded. The Texas Company was formed on January 1, 2014. Organization costs of $10,000 were incurred at the time and are being amortized over a 60-month period.
6. The ending merchandise inventory is $130,000.

Other Adjustment Data

On December 31, 2016, journalize and post the estimated federal income tax. Periodically, Congress changes corporate income tax rates. As of this writing, the federal rates are shown in the table below (*Hint:* Remember to round all computations to the nearest whole dollar.)

Taxable Income		Tax Rate
First	$50,000	15 percent
Next	$25,000	25 percent
Next	$25,000	34 percent
Next	$235,000	39 percent
Over	$335,000	See Internal Revenue Service publications for taxable income of more than $335,000.

Required:

Round all computations to the nearest whole dollar.

1. Restore the Mini Practice Set 3.The Texas Company.QBM file.
2. Journalize and post the transactions on page 126-127 in the general journal. (*Hint:* Journalize and post the January 5 through December 30 transactions *and* the December 31, 2016 summary operating transactions.)
3. Print the January 1 to December 31, 2016 trial balance (unadjusted).
4. Backup. The suggested filename is **Mini Practice Set 3.December**.
5. Journalize and post the adjusting entries. (Refer to the year-end adjustments on page 127.)
6. Print the December 31, 2016 adjusting journal entry.
7. Print the January 1 to December 31, 2016 adjusted trial balance.
8. Print the January 1 to December 31, 2016 Profit & Loss statement. Use a blank piece of paper or the *Working Papers* to prepare a summary income statement. For the summary income statement, refer to QuickBooks' P&L.

   For the summary income statement, the January 1 merchandise inventory amount is $150,000; the December 31, merchandise inventory is $130,000. Since merchandise inventory is an asset, QB shows the merchandise inventory balance on the balance sheet. For that reason, the net income amount will differ on QuickBooks' P&L and the manually prepared summary income statement. The net income difference is the same as the difference between the December 31 and January 1 balance in the merchandise inventory accou nt.

January 1, 2016, merchandise inventory	$150,000
Minus December 31, 2016, merchandise inventory	− 130,000
Difference	$ 20,000

QuickBooks' P&L net income	$165,815
Minus Summary Income Statement	145,815
Difference	$ 20,000

9. Use a blank piece of paper or the *Working Papers* to prepare a statement of retained earnings for the year ended December 31, 2016.
10. Print the balance sheet for the year ended December 31, 2016.
11. Backup. The suggested filename is **Mini Practice Set 3.Adjusted**.
12. Journalize and post the closing entries.
13. Print the January 5 to December 31, 2016 journal.
14. Print the January 1 to December 31, 2016 general ledger.
15. Backup. The suggested filename is **Mini Practice Set 3.Closed**.
16. **Analyze:** Assume that the firm declared and issued a 3:1 stock split of common stock in 2016. What is the effect on total par value?

Chapter 27
Job Order Cost Accounting

In Chapter 27 of *College Accounting, 14e*, there is one QuickBooks problem.

> Problem 27.1A SoCal Trailers Co.: Recording purchase and issuance of direct and indirect materials, recording labor costs, applying overhead, computing overapplied or underapplied overhead, recording cost of jobs completed and cost of goods sold.

Chapter 27's QuickBooks activities demonstrate how to:

- Restore one QuickBooks problem template.
- Journalize and post transactions.
- Print the journal.
- Complete Problem 27.1A.

GETTING STARTED: Problem 27.1A

Follow these steps to start QuickBooks and restore the Problem 27.1A.SoCal Trailers Co.QBM file.

Instructions:

1. Start QuickBooks.
2. If the menu bar shows a company name, click File; Open or Restore Company.
3. The Open or Restore Company window appears. Select Restore a portable file.
4. Click [Next]. The Open Portable Company File window appears. In the Look in field, go to the appropriate location for the Problem 27.1A.SoCal Trailers Co.QBM file. Click on the file to highlight it. Click [Open]. (*Hint:* You can also double-click on the file name.)
5. The Open or Restore Company window appears. Click [Next].
6. The Save Company File as window appears. Accept the default file name or change it slightly. Click [Save]. When SoCal Trailers Co - QuickBooks Accountant 2014 appears, the file is restored.
7. Continue with the next section "My Company."

My Company

Before recording transactions for the SoCal Trailers Co. look at the My Company information included on the Problem 27.1A.SoCal Trailers Co.QBM file.

1. From the Icon Bar, select ![My Company]. (*Or,* from the menu bar, select Company; My Company.) The My Company window appears.

2. To add your name to the Company Name field, click ![pencil icon]. Close the My Company window.

In April 2016, SoCal Trailers Co. had the following cost data. Use April 30 as the date.

Cost Data

1. Raw materials costing $92,000 were purchased.
2. Raw materials costing $91,000 were used: direct materials, $85,000; indirect materials $6,000.
3. Factory wages of $72,000 were incurred: direct labor $60,000; indirect labor $12,000. Social security tax deductions were $4,464, Medicare tax deductions were $1,044, federal income tax deductions were $10,800.
4. Other overhead costs of $29,000 were incurred. (Credit Accounts Payable.)
5. Estimated manufacturing overhead costs were applied to jobs in production at the rate of 75 percent of direct labor costs.
6. Finished goods costing $160,000 were transferred from production to the warehouse.
7. The cost of goods sold was $130,000.
8. Sales on account for the month were $220,000.

Required:

1. Restore the Problem 27.1A.SoCal Trailers Co.QBM file.
2. Journalize and post the transactions. Date the transactions April 30, 2016. Refer to the Cost Data section, 1-8, above.
3. Print the April 30, 2016 journal.
4. Use a blank piece of paper or the *Working Papers* to compute the amount of overapplied or underapplied overhead for the month. The report title is Manufacturing Overhead Computations for the month ended April 30, 2016.
5. Use a blank piece of paper or the *Working Papers* to prepare a partial income statement for April. Adjust the Cost of Goods Sold for any overapplied or underapplied overhead. (*Hint:* You may want to refer QuickBooks' profit and loss report.)
6. Back up. The suggested file name is **Problem 27.1A.QBM**.
7. **Analyze:** Based on the partial income statement you have prepared, what portion of each sales dollar is realized as gross profit? Use a blank piece of paper or the *Working Papers* to complete the analysis question.

Appendix A

Troubleshooting and QuickBooks Tips

Appendix A, Troubleshooting and QuickBooks Tips, includes the following.

QUICKBOOKS FOR THE MAC

To learn about Windows operating system compatibility with the Mac, go online to http://www.apple.com/findouthow/mac/#windowsmac. Every new Mac lets you install and run Windows at native speeds, using a built-in utility called Boot Camp.

Setup is simple and safe for your Mac files. After you've completed the installation, you can boot up your Mac using either OS X or Windows. Or if you want to run Windows and Mac applications at the same time — without rebooting — you can install Windows using VMware Fusion (http://www.vmware.com/products/fusion/overview.html) or Parallels software (http://www.parallels.com/products/desktop/).

The 160-day software CD included with the *Student Guide for QuickBooks 2014* is PC compatible (Windows 8, 7, and Vista).

SET UP FOLDERS FOR DATA MANAGEMENT

You may want to organize QuickBooks' file types in separate folders. QuickBooks' file types include portable backup files (.QBM extensions) and company files (.QBW extensions).

How Do I Show File Extensions?

To show files extensions, follow these steps.

1. Right-click on the <Start> button; left-click Explore. (The selection in Windows 7 is Open Windows Explorer.)

2. Click on the Organize down-arrow. Select Folder and Search Options. Click on the View tab.

3. Uncheck Hide extensions for known file types.

☐ Hide extensions for known file types

4. Click <OK> to close the Folder Options window.

5. Close Windows Explorer.

QuickBooks Problem Templates Folder

The problem template files are in a folder labeled QuickBooks Problem Templates.

QuickBooks Problem Templates
File folder

Each QuickBooks Problem Template file ends in a QBM extension. In QuickBooks, files that end in a QBM extension are identified as portable files. In the *Student Guide*, portable files are used for both the template files and saved or backed up files. The problem template files included on the QuickBooks Templates CD are shown on the next page.

```
Mini Practice Set 1.Wells' Consulting Services.QBM        Problem 15.1A.Montana Leather Products.QBM
Mini Practice Set 2.The Fashion Rack.QBM                  Problem 15.2A.Lucero Company.QBM
Mini Practice Set 3.The Texas Company.QBM                 Problem 15.4A.Pullman Company.QBM
Problem 04.2A.Satillo Richey.QBM                          Problem 16.2A.Dennis Company.QBM
Problem 04.4A.Farmers Market and Repair Shop.QBM          Problem 16.5A.Reliable Company.QBM
Problem 05.4A.Judge Creative Designs.QBM                  Problem 19.2A.Oatis and Thomas Angler's Outpost.QBM
Problem 06.1A.Consumer Research Associates.QBM            Problem 19.4A.Larry's Antiques.QBM
Problem 06.2A.The King Group.QBM                          Problem 19.5A.Adams Pharmacy.QBM
Problem 07.1A.Best Appliances.QBM                         Problem 20.4A.Denzel Corporation.QBM
Problem 07.2A.Towncenter Furniture.QBM                    Problem 20.5A.Jaguar Corporation.QBM
Problem 07.4A.Bella Floral Designs.QBM                    Problem 21.1A.Divad Corporation.QBM
Problem 08.1A.Digital World.QBM                           Problem 21.3A.Solomon Corporation.QBM
Problem 08.3A.The English Garden Shop.QBM                 Problem 21.4A.Willy Corporation.QBM
Problem 08.4A.Office Plus.QBM                             Problem 22.1A.Carlie Services Inc.QBM
Problem 09.1A.Entertainment Inc.QBM                       Problem 22.4A.New Computer Technology, Inc.QBM
Problem 09.3A.Awesome Sounds.QBM                          Problem 27.1A.SoCal Trailers Co.QBM
Problem 09.4A.Bike and Hike Outlet.QBM
Problem 11.2A.Mark Consulting Company.QBM
Problem 12.2A.Sean McConnell.QBM
Problem 13.1A.Quality Hardwoods Company.QBM
Problem 13.5A.Victoria Company.QBM

37 items
```

QuickBooks Company Files Folder

You may want to set up a folder for QuickBooks' company files. QuickBooks' company files end in the extension .QBW.

Before restoring files, set up a folder labeled QuickBooks Company Files_QBW.

QuickBooks Company Files_QBW
File folder

When you restore files in QuickBooks, a Save Company File as window appears. In the Save in field, select the QuickBooks Company Files_QBW folder.

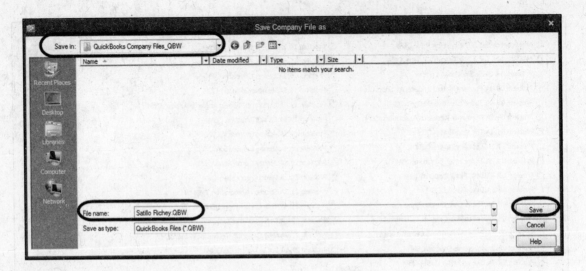

By saving the company files to its own folder, you store the company files (.QBW files) in a different location than the problem template files (.QBM extensions).

When a company is opened in QuickBooks, the following file extensions are associated with that company file:

1. .QBW: QuickBooks working file or company file
2. .DSN: Database source name
3. .ND: network data file
4. .TLG: transaction logs

Saved Problem Files Folder

After completing a problem, you could save the backed up files in a separate folder labeled Saved Problem Files.

Saved Problem Files
File folder

If all the problems are completed in the *Student Guide for QuickBooks 2014,* the backed up files include the files shown on the next page.

Mini Practice Set 1.Adjusted.QBM	Problem 07.4A.QBM	Problem 16.2A.QBM
Mini Practice Set 1.Closed.QBM	Problem 08.1A.QBM	Problem 16.5A.QBM
Mini Practice Set 1.January.QBM	Problem 08.3A.QBM	Problem 19.2A.QBM
Mini Practice Set 2.Adjusted.QBM	Problem 08.4A.QBM	Problem 19.4A.QBM
Mini Practice Set 2.Closed.QBM	Problem 09.1A.QBM	Problem 19.5A.QBM
Mini Practice Set 2.October.QBM	Problem 09.3A.QBM	Problem 20.4A.QBM
Mini Practice Set 3.Adjusted.QBM	Problem 09.4A.QBM	Problem 20.5A.QBM
Mini Practice Set 3.Closed.QBM	Problem 11.2A.QBM	Problem 21.1A.QBM
Mini Practice Set 3.December.QBM	Problem 12.2A.QBM	Problem 21.3A.QBM
Problem 04.2A.QBM	Problem 13.1A.QBM	Problem 21.4A.QBM
Problem 04.4A.QBM	Problem 13.5A.Adjusted.QBM	Problem 22.1A.2016.QBM
Problem 05.4A.QBM	Problem 13.5A.Reversed.QBM	Problem 22.1A.2017.QBM
Problem 06.1A.QBM	Problem 15.1A.Adjusted.QBM	Problem 22.4A.Bond Retirement.QBM
Problem 06.2A.Adjusted.QBM	Problem 15.1A.QBM	Problem 22.4A.Face Value.QBM
Problem 06.2A.Closed.QBM	Problem 15.2A.December 2016.QBM	Problem 27.1A.QBM
Problem 07.1A.QBM	Problem 15.2A.June 2017.QBM	
Problem 07.2A.QBM	Problem 15.4A.QBM	

49 items

Types of Backup Files

QuickBooks includes three types of backup files:

1. Backup copy (.QBB extensions)
2. Portable company file (.QBM extensions)
3. Accountant's copy (.QBX or .QBA extensions)

To back up a file in QuickBooks, select File; Create Copy. The Save Copy or Backup window appears with three backup selections. Select Portable company file.

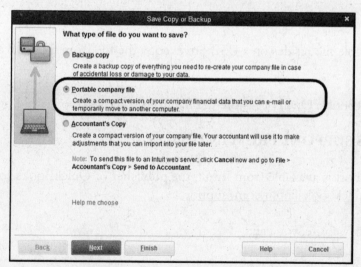

In the *Student Guide*, the method shown for backing up is the Portable company file selection. The other two files types, Backup copy and Accountant's copy, save larger files.

TROUBLESHOOTING BACKUP AND RESTORE: USING USB DRIVES

USB drives use different files systems. To see your USB drive's file system, right-click on the drive letter, left-click Properties, then select the General tab. Some USB drives are more reliable than others. If you are experiencing difficulty using a USB drive when either restoring from or backing up to it, use your Desktop instead. In other words, backup to your desktop first, then copy the file to a USB drive. Do the same thing in reverse when you want to restore a file. Copy the file from the USB drive to your desktop, then restore the file from your desktop instead of from a USB drive.

Create Copy or Backup: Portable Company Files

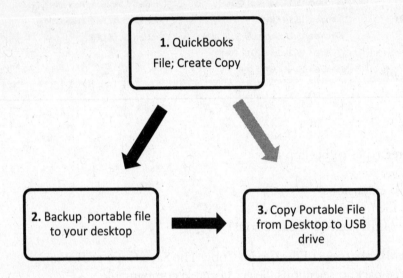

Restore a file

1. If the portable file resides on a USB drive, copy the file from the USB drive to your desktop.

2. Start QuickBooks. Open or restore the file from your desktop instead of the USB drive.

QUICKBOOKS SUPPORT FROM INTUIT

QuickBooks support is available from Intuit, the publisher of QuickBooks software, at http://support.quickbooks.intuit.com/support.

From the support website, you can:

- Get install help.
- Get downloads & updates
- Go to new user resource center.
- Type search words or error message number.

HELP WINDOWS

Use the <F1> function key for Help from any QuickBooks window. When you press <F1>, a Have a Question window appears. In the example below, <F1> was selected from the Home page.

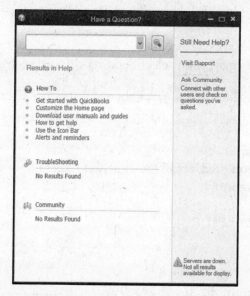

You can search help, type a word in the Search field, Visit Support, or Ask Community.

When the Chart of Accounts is selected, then <F1>, context-sensitive help appears.

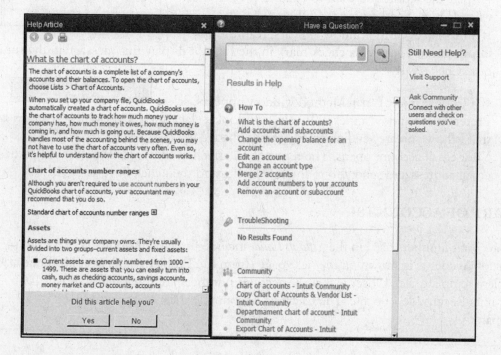

USE EXCEL WITH QUICKBOOKS

Your instructor may want you to email QuickBooks assignments completed in the *Student Guide*. QuickBooks includes a way to export reports to Excel.

Follow these steps to export a QuickBooks report to Excel.

1. Display the report for the appropriate date.
2. You have two choices: E-mail, then select Send report as Excel; *or,* Export. In these steps Export is selected. Click [Excel ▼], then select either Create a New Worksheet or Update Existing Worksheet.
3. The Send Report to Excel window appears. You can Create a new worksheet or add to an existing workbook.
4. Save the Excel file. If requested, email the attached Excel file to your instructor.
5. Close the QuickBooks report.

E-MAIL REPORT AS A PDF FILE

You can email reports as PDF files.

When you send a report as a PDF file, the report is attached to an email message. If you do not have Acrobat Reader, you can download it for free from www.adobe.com.

1. Display the report you want to email as a PDF file.
2. Click E-mail, Send report as PDF.
3. If an Email Security window appears, read the information. Then put a check mark in the Do not display this message in the future box. Click <OK>.
4. If a Choose Your Email Method window appears, select [Setup my email now]. The Preferences window appears. If using Outlook, select it. (If Web Mail is selected and that is how you are sending email, do not change it.)
5. Your email account opens. The report is an attached PDF file. Type the recipient's email address and send. Go to the File menu, and then click Save as PDF.

CHART OF ACCOUNTS

The account numbers used in the *Student Guide* include three-digit numbers. An example Chart of Accounts is shown on the next page (from the Problem 04.2A.Satillo Richey.QBM problem template file). Observe that the account numbers are three digits--Cash, 101; Accounts Receivable, 106, etc. The Chart of Accounts is a list of accounts used by a company.

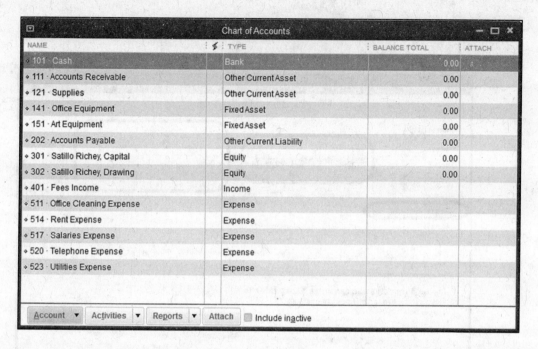

When companies are created, QuickBooks automatically sets up some accounts. The accounts that QuickBooks automatically sets up have five-digit numbers. When you display the general ledger, you will see all the accounts. The general ledger is a record containing all accounts (with amounts) for a business.

An example of an account that QuickBooks automatically sets up is Account No. 24000 - Payroll Liabilities.

FILTERING REPORTS

There are numerous ways to print or display reports. For example, you can filter reports for the type of transaction.

After completing the October transactions for Mini Practice Set 2, The Fashion Rack, let's say you want to look at the vendor bills paid.

1. Restore the Mini Practice Set 2.October.QBM file.
2. From the Report Center or menu bar, select Reports; Accountant & Taxes, Journal. Display the 10/1/2016 o 10/31/2016 Journal.
3. Select Customize Report. The Modify Report: Journal window appears. Select the Filters tab.

4. In the Filter list, select Transaction Type. In the Transaction Type field, select Bill Payment.

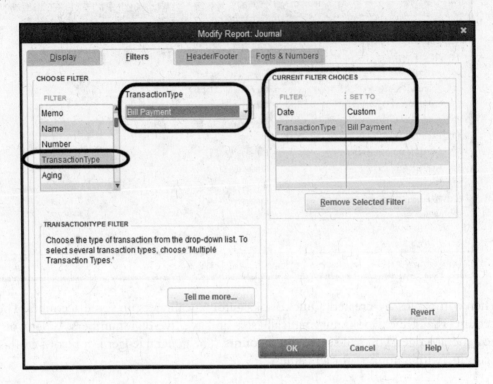

5. Click <OK>. The Journal appears showing vendor payments only. The Journal window is shown below.

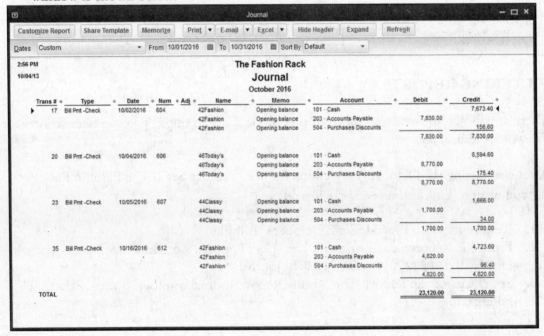

ADD SHORTCUTS TO THE ICON BAR

1. From the menu bar, select View; Customize Icon Bar. Click [Add...]. You can also delete shortcuts that you do not want to appear on the Icon Bar.
2. The Add Icon Bar Item window appears. Select an item to add. Observe the Label and Description field identifies the item. You can also customize the label and description. Click [OK].
3. The Customize Icon Bar window appears. To reorder the icons, drag an icon's diamond up or down to the position you want.

ICON BAR LOCATION

The Icon Bar can be located on the top, left, or it can be hidden. To change the location of the Icon Bar, from the menu bar, select View.

The Left Icon Bar is selected. Other selections include Top Icon Bar or Hide Icon Bar.

UNINSTALL QUICKBOOKS AND REMOVE ALL QUICKBOOKS FILES AND FOLDERS

It is sometimes necessary to uninstall QuickBooks, rename installation files left behind, and then reinstall QuickBooks. This may be required when a QuickBooks function is damaged or when simply reinstalling QuickBooks does not correct an issue. This process is called a **Clean Install** or **Clean Uninstall**.

Note: Be sure to have your QuickBooks download file or your installation CD and installation license available before uninstalling QuickBooks.

Read the instructions on this website to determine which uninstall method you prefer http://support.quickbooks.intuit.com/support/Articles/HOW12212.

TOGGLE QUICKBOOKS TO THE ANOTHER EDITION

The student trial version software, included with the *Student Guide*, can be used on one computer for 160 days.

Before following these steps, check with your instructor for his or her preference. The software site license purchased by the school and the 160-day CD included with the *Student Guide* are the same software version.

1. From the menu bar, select File; Toggle to Another Edition. The Select QuickBooks Industry-Specific Edition window appears. Select QuickBooks Pro.

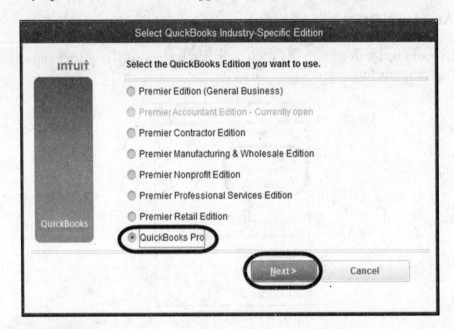

2. Click Next > and the version of QuickBooks changes to the Pro.

UPDATE COMPANY FILE TO NEW VERSION

Problem template files are upward but not downward compatible. This means that the problem template files can be used with QuickBooks 2014 and higher versions (QB 2015 and higher), but <u>not</u> lower versions of QuickBooks (2013 and lower).

QuickBooks 2014 is included with the *Student Guide*. The problem templates were created with the 2014 version. If you are using a higher version of QuickBooks, for example QB 2015, an Update Company File to New Version window appears when you are restoring problem templates. Follow these steps to update the file to a higher version of QuickBooks.

1. Click on the box next to I understand that my company file will be updated to this new version of QuickBooks.

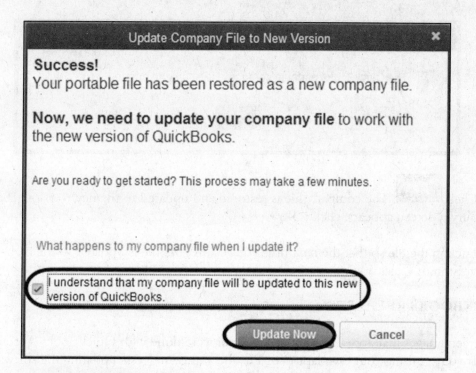

2. Click 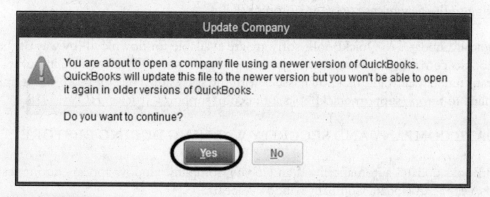. The Update Company window appears.

3. Click [Yes]. When the scale on the Updating Data window is complete, the company file is updated.
4. The QuickBooks Information window appears.

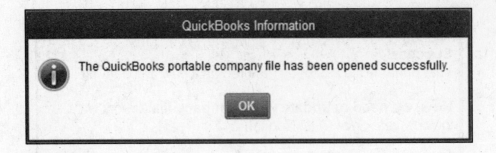

5. Click [OK]. The company file is restored and updated to the new version. If a Survey screen appears, click <No>.

6. Backup the file so that the next time you restore, the file is updated to the higher version of QuickBooks.

QUICKBOOKS RELEASES

The screen images that appear in the *Student Guide* were done with QuickBooks Accountant 2014. If you are using your own laptop or PC, the author suggests updating the software. When you compare screen images with the *Student Guide*, you may notice some differences. For example, if you are using QuickBooks 2014 at school and the computer lab is <u>not</u> updating the software, this could result in some differences in screen images, *or* if you are not updating to the new release on your laptop or PC.

Periodically, updates to QuickBooks software are available for download (by way of the quickbooks.com website) or internally through your software. These updates improve program functionality and fix known issues with the software. To learn more about updates go online to <u>http://support.quickbooks.intuit.com/support/Articles/HOW12418</u>.

UPDATE COMPANY AND SECURITY WARNING DURING RESTORE

QuickBooks updates automatically. If an Update Company window appears during restore, click <Yes>. An Update Company window appears.

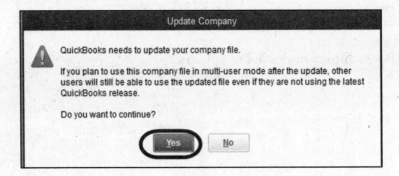

If a Security Warning window appears, Click <Yes>.

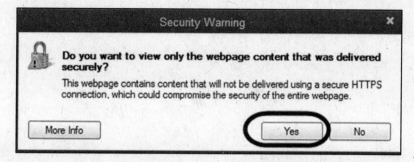

You can press the function key <F2> to see the QuickBooks release being used.

Your release number may differ. If some of your screen images look different when compared to the illustrations in the *Student Guide*, you or the computer lab may not have updated QuickBooks. For more information, refer to page 144, QuickBooks Releases.